THE
PAYOFF

THE
PAYOFF

WHY WALL STREET ALWAYS WINS

JEFF CONNAUGHTON

PROSPECTA PRESS

Published by
PROSPECTA PRESS
P.O. Box 3131, Westport, CT 06880
(203) 454-4454
www.prospectapress.com

For information about permission
to reproduce selections from this book, write to:
Anderson Literary Management LLC
12 W. 19th Street, Second Floor, New York, NY 10011
(Attention: Permissions Department)

Book design by Barbara Aronica-Buck
Cover design by Carly Schnur

Paperback ISBN: 978-1-935212-96-6
E-book ISBN: 978-1-935212-97-3

First hardcover printing: September 2012
First ebook publication: August 2012

Printed in the United States of America

FIRST EDITION

10 9 8 7 6 5 4 3 2 1

To my parents

CONTENTS

THE
PAYOFF

PROLOGUE

IN DECEMBER 2007, less than a year before America's financial crisis, I had no special reason, despite my experience, to know what lay ahead. At the time, I was serving as a volunteer in Joe Biden's presidential campaign in Waterloo, Iowa. An apt place, I thought, for what I knew was my last stand for Biden, for whom I had worked on and off for twenty-three years. Presidential campaigns are often exercises in self-delusion, for the candidate and his supporters, but up to the finish I could still convince myself, at least occasionally, that my old hero had a chance, despite what the world was telling me. I distinctly remember the day when Ted Kaufman (Biden's long-time chief of staff and my former boss in Biden's Senate office) and Beau Biden (Biden's oldest son) gave a passionate pitch on a conference call from headquarters to sixty-eight political captains across our region. After the call, I told Ted—a wise and savvy political veteran—that for a second he even had me believing him. "In a presidential campaign, you're either faking it or you're dead," Ted said. The faking came to an end when only six people

1

stood in the Biden corner on caucus night at the high school I was monitoring. Barack Obama had nearly eighty, Hillary Clinton about sixty. Elsewhere in the state, Biden's defeat was equally crushing.

Afterwards, I left the campaign to fly to Costa Rica, where I was thinking about building a house, to recharge. My architect and a developer joined me for dinner at a hotel restaurant in Punta Islita. Both were Americans, each a few more years into middle age than me. We had barely ordered dinner when the developer said he had just returned from New York City where he was involved with the loan committees of Merrill Lynch and Lehman Brothers. "Both companies are technically insolvent." Startled, I put down my glass. "What? I don't believe it." This was two months before Bear Stearns began to falter and fail. "If that's true we're all in a world of shit," I said. I remember my words exactly. I couldn't believe what the man was saying. I'd been trained in business and law school to believe that corporate governance worked. Even though I knew Wall Street held Washington in a perpetual half nelson, I still believed our laws would prevent hidden catastrophes and blatant fraud. Our system is based on full disclosure of independently audited financial statements combined with oversight and enforcement from the Securities and Exchange Commission. How could it be that two major Wall Street firms were "technically insolvent" but the world didn't know about it?

The developer went even further: "I predict we're going into a three-year recession." I was flabbergasted.

This man had just stepped off a plane from New York, where he was connected at the heart of the world's financial center, and he was telling me that we were headed toward an economic disaster. Rather than take the tip and modify my investments, I argued with him that it couldn't be true. My own stock portfolio was globally diversified, and I thought, at worst, the market might face a 10 percent correction.

Then Bear Stearns failed in March 2008. The markets began to gyrate. Still, our government leaders continued to make reassuring statements. I came to believe that the economy and stock market might be heading for a significant pullback, but considered it nothing to lose sleep over.

I should've known that the legal and regulatory system meant to protect us had rotted away. For more than twenty years, I'd seen up close how Wall Street manipulates government, the revolving door, the shared mindset, how siding with the Establishment is almost always the best career move.

I had started my career on Wall Street before moving to Washington in 1987 to work on Biden's first presidential campaign. I had worked on Capitol Hill and walked by Wall Street lobbyists camped in the hallway. As a lawyer in the White House, I'd personally seen President Bill Clinton steamrolled by Wall Street (and by its biggest booster, the most Machiavellian of United States senators, Chris Dodd) circa 1995. Dodd had led Congress to overturn President Clinton's veto of the Private Securities Litigation Reform Act, which he and the Republicans had drafted to gut the class-action securities-fraud laws. It was the only Clinton veto given the back-of-the-hand by two-thirds of Congress. And it was my first taste of how Wall Street had come to own Washington.

I understood Wall Street's methods of seducing senators, members of Congress, and regulators because I'd done it myself as a lobbyist. After I left government, I practiced appellate litigation, but soon drifted into a legislative and regulatory law practice with Jack Quinn (former White House Counsel and, before that, Vice President Al Gore's chief of staff). A few years later, Jack and I co-founded Quinn Gillespie & Associates with Ed Gillespie (former House Majority Leader Dick Armey's communications director and later chairman of the Republican National Committee). It went on to become one of the most successful—and profitable—bipartisan public affairs firms in Washington. For twelve years, I developed and implemented legislative and regulatory campaign strategies for corporate clients, including broker-dealers, banks, accountants, insurance firms, and Silicon Valley. During my years as a lobbyist, I made a big pile of money, enough to have a house in Georgetown, a speedboat on the Chesapeake, and soon—I hoped—an oceanfront home in Costa Rica.

For Biden people, whose hopes had been crushed during the primary season, the 2008 Democratic Convention was surreal. After all those decades, all those conventions Biden had attended, all the work we had put into two presidential campaigns—for naught—and then Barack Obama wakes up one day and says to Joe, "You're going to be the vice presidential candidate." The night of Biden's acceptance speech, the convention suite was a scene of triumph for Biden's family and long-standing supporters. All of a sudden, Joe Biden, Jill, their children Beau, Hunter, and Ashley, and their families, were all on the stage. It was the party of a lifetime.

Outside the convention hall, fewer were celebrating. In fact, the festivities were about to end. After a summer of Lehman Brothers executives publicly assuring investors that their company was sound, the end came: On September 15, 2008, Lehman Brothers declared bankruptcy, causing the Dow to plunge. My conversation in Costa Rica hit me like an anvil. The developer clearly had been right, apparently privy to inside information that should've been shared with the world. How could that have happened? In hindsight, I wished he'd reached across the dinner table, grabbed me by the lapels, and said, "I know you just met me, but think hard about this: I just came back from meetings at Merrill Lynch and Lehman Brothers. Both firms are technically insolvent. Believe me, you need to act. Sell everything you own before it's too late."

The two months that followed the Lehman bankruptcy were a financial catastrophe for the country (and for me). Obama and Biden were elected in a climate of economic fear. And I strongly suspected that at least a few Wall Street insiders had known it was coming.

By the Friday after Election Day, 2008, I was back
on board with Biden, taking the train to Wilmington
for a meeting with the Vice President-Elect to discuss
the transition. I was lugging eight copies of a massive
VP Bible, a comprehensive manual for establishing and
running a vice-presidency, which Ted and I had put together. It included organizational charts, budgets,
schematics of office space in the Old Executive Office
Building, and descriptions of previous VP models.
(Walter Mondale was credited with defining the modern vice presidency, as Jimmy Carter had empowered
him to play an advisory role in virtually every area; Dan
Quayle had carved out a couple of areas of responsibility for himself; Al Gore was considered a hybrid, involved in all decisions, but also taking the lead on
environmental, telecommunications policy, and rein-
venting government.)

Sitting at the table with the Vice President-Elect
were his wife, Jill, as well as loyalists such as Ron Klain,
Mike Donilon, Mark Gitenstein, Tony Blinken, Dennis Toner, Ted, and me. Biden had committed a gaffe
in the final days of the campaign, saying it was likely
that a country hostile to the United States would pur-
posely take action to test Obama's foreign-policy mettle
in the first six months of his presidency. Biden told us
that Obama had called him and told him sharply that
he didn't need public tutoring: "I don't need you acting
like you're my Henry Higgins." Biden said his private
reaction was, "Whoa. Where did this come from? This
is clearly a guy who could restrict my role to attending

state funerals or just put me in a closet for four years." Biden added: "I'm going to have to earn his trust, but I'm not going to grovel to this guy. My manhood is not negotiable." It was heady stuff for me.

We turned to a discussion of the inaugural and who should be in charge for the Biden team. Ted suggested me, without any prior discussion with Biden or the group. I knew immediately that because I'd been a lobbyist, this notion was unlikely to stand for long, though no one wanted to embarrass me in front of the group. Biden simply turned to me and said, "Okay, Jeff, but I want you to promise that you'll listen to me on all decisions. Some guy who picked me up when I was hitch-hiking might mean more to me than someone who raised $100K, do you get what I mean?" I assured him I'd defer to him on all those decisions. I suspected that Biden saw me fundamentally as a fundraiser who would give undue precedence to those who had helped raised money.

I was right. Obama's anti-lobbying jihad, which had begun during the campaign, returned with renewed fervor in the early days of the transition. My days in the Biden inner circle looked numbered. John Podesta, whom, oddly enough, I'd met twenty years earlier when he was lobbying me, was head of the transition, and he announced publicly that no one who had worked as a registered lobbyist in the past two years would be welcome in the Obama administration. If we lose good people because of this, he said, "so be it."

Soon, Ted asked me to lunch. Before he could get

out a word, I said, "Let me have the dignity of resigning as chair of the Biden inaugural team before you dismiss me." It was even worse: I was off the transition team entirely. It didn't seem fair. Biden had never helped me once as a lobbyist, yet I was paying the price.

"I have the perfect solution for you," Ted said. Biden had suggested that Ted take his place in the Senate for the two years before Delaware would hold a special election. That was truly great news. Ted had advised Biden during his entire Senate career, and for almost twenty years had taught a course about Congress at Duke Law School. "Ted, you'll be a great senator," I said. Ted went on to say that if he became senator, he wanted me as his chief of staff. That didn't really come as a surprise. More than twenty years ago, during my first Biden campaign, someone had described me as "a tool of Ted's will." I'd long been Ted's implementer-in-chief.

The two-year term did have a simple elegance to it. I was excited, suddenly a believer once more. And I had a mission from the beginning. I was livid about the financial crisis and Wall Street's role in it. Ted was too. The economy was imploding because of Wall Street excess (and likely: malfeasance), and in the run-up to the financial meltdown the ruling class in Washington had done nothing to stop it. My newly acquired wealth had already been cut by more than a third. I was finding it all too easy to channel the anger of the millions of Americans whose 401(k)s had taken a proportionate whack.

I wanted to be back in government. Yes, I had gone along with corporate lobbying and done my share of tipping the scale in favor of business interests. Yes, with my Biden connections, I could be more successful than ever as a lobbyist. But the market crash and subsequent recession had shattered my faith in the law and U.S. institutions. It was a seismic disturbance, a time of national crisis, and I had spent decades of my life trying to get Biden in a position of national power. Somewhat naïvely, I envisioned Ted and me as Vice President Biden's emissaries in the Senate, an extension of the Obama-Biden team.

So Ted and I made a pact: In the Senate, we'd spend two years fighting for accountability for the financial crisis and for structural reforms that would ensure there'd never be another one. He became a United States senator, and I became his top aide.

And that's when the hard part started. For two years, Senator Kaufman and I kicked Wall Street in the groin every day. We loudly advocated the prosecution of financial fraudsters, prodded the SEC to do something—anything—about high-frequency trading and the vertiginous market swings it was causing, and pushed for meaningful financial regulatory reform. Despite our nearly fanatical dedication, we and other reformers failed. To date, there have been no high-profile Wall Street prosecutions for financial wrongdoing. The stock market has become even more volatile and dominated by computer-driven trading. Too-big-to-fail banks continue to act lawlessly, teeter on the brink, and destabilize the global economy. The post-crisis regulatory reforms (particularly, the Dodd-Frank Act) were and are being written by over-matched regulators with the help of Wall Street lawyers instead of by the elected representatives of Americans, a substantial majority of whom support rules to rein in Wall Street excesses.

I can't explain why President Obama (and Vice President Biden) have failed to support stronger enforcement efforts or financial reform—or describe the institutional resistance that pushed back against Kaufman, me, and others—as well as a historian or political scientist or, for that matter, a sociologist could. As someone who served in mid-level positions in government and lobbying for more than two decades, however, I can give an insider's view. It took stepping through the looking glass and back into government during a catastrophe to see what I'd become and to realize just how poorly Washington's culture and institutions now perform. The failure to prosecute Wall Street fraud and enact strong reform during Ted's two years in office continues to have dire repercussions for the American economy, the very credibility of finance, and trust in the rule of law.

The onset of the Great Recession should've been a moment when reformers realized the financial elite's grip on Washington had become too strong, as when Teddy Roosevelt stood up to the trusts and FDR cracked down on Wall Street. Instead, Obama and Biden gave the problem a sideways glance and then delegated the solutions to the same circle of Wall Street-Washington technocrats who had brought the financial disaster upon us in the first place. Left on their own, the reformers in Congress—mired in Washington's bog of near-corruption, and without any help from a Republican Party more eager to pursue Wall Street for fundraising than reform—could produce only the slightest momentum for change.

Money is the basis of almost all relationships in DC. And, in a nutshell, this is why our political campaign system and DC's mushrooming Permanent Class—who alternate between government jobs and lawyering, influence-peddling and finance—mean Wall Street always wins. The rest of the country may be divided into red and blue, but DC is green (that is, covered in money), and cheerfully so. Nationally, we're descending further into bitter partisan warfare, while in Washington, professional Democrats and Republicans gleefully join together to work for those special interests that can afford to pay them. Among the political class, the center may be disappearing, but at my old lobbying firm, Quinn Gillespie & Associates, it's holding together quite well.

During my twenty-three years in Washington, I saw government attract thousands of idealistic, energetic young people from across the country and lead many of them to make compromises that drew them deeper into a corrupt system. The initial magnetism of politics is far different from its day-to-day reality; for most people, careerism and the weight of years inevitably crushes idealism. Those years changed me, as well. I came to DC a Democrat and left a plutocrat.

With his term nearly over, Senator Kaufman suggested we start a not-for-profit to keep fighting the Washington-Wall Street nexus on behalf of the rule of law and the average investor. For me, it was a Pogo moment. I said: "Ted, we've met the enemy, and the enemy is us." I didn't want to stay in DC and keep losing in hand-to-hand combat against Wall Street (or worse, rejoin the Permanent Class). I sold my Georgetown house and packed my bags so that I could leave Washington on Ted's last day in office. It was time for a strategic retreat.

Today, as a private citizen living in Savannah, Georgia, I hope more Americans will work to change the corrupted system that now governs us. It's time people understand why—and how—Wall Street always wins. It's not a tale of bags filled with cash and quid pro quos. It's more subtle than that, and in some ways best told by my own personal story and the compromises I made along the way. Party cohesion and the desire to make a munificent living in DC go a long way to enforce silence. Yet I'm willing to burn every bridge. Now that I've mutinied and fled to a remote place, I want to set flame to the ship that would take me back there. I have to build a life—and discover a different way of living—on Pitcairn Island.

1:

THE ACCIDENTAL
SENATOR

ON NOVEMBER 24, 2008, Governor Ruth Ann Minner of Delaware announced her intention to appoint Ted Kaufman to Joe Biden's Senate seat. Upon accepting the appointment, Ted made it clear that he'd hold the office for only two years; he absolutely wouldn't run in the special election that would determine his successor. He thought it best for the voters to pick Delaware's next U.S. senator, without his using the advantages of incumbency to try to hold the seat.

He knew that, if he planned to run for election, he'd have to spend almost half his time preparing for a future campaign, and most of that working to raise the enormous number of dollars it takes to compete in a Senate election. After having been in and around the Senate for almost thirty-six years, he wanted to enjoy being a full-time senator—and explode out of the blocks for a two-year sprint on the issues he cared deeply about. He didn't want to fundraise, play politics, or avoid making enemies. He wanted to be his own man, completely independent. In Washington: a *rara avis*.

Ted was truly motivated to work hard and make a difference. Initially, few outside Delaware perceived this, which, in hindsight, may have been a good thing. Many in Delaware respected him, but from the beginning they labeled him a placeholder—and, worse, a seat warmer—for Beau Biden, then the Delaware attorney general. Everyone saw Ted as the guy Biden most trusted not to run against his son in the special election. Biden, not known for his tact or sensitivity to the positions of others, didn't help matters when he issued a long statement describing his son as, potentially, a great U.S. senator.

Ted had to defend himself against the placeholder label in every early media interview. I could tell the misperception stung, but, if anything, the denigration and condescension made him even more determined to disprove the cynics and make his days in office count. He was going to swing a big bat if he could get his hands around one. He told the Delaware media: "I'm not about having a bunch of bills with 'Kaufman' on them. What I'm about is, at the end of two years, being able to say that I tried as hard as I could to help make the country a better place." For those who know Ted, that wasn't blarney. It was as if he'd been waiting all those years, watching government and the country change, accumulating knowledge, storing up his life's purpose until he had the opportunity to harness it to a just cause.

Ted Kaufman is, indeed, a humanitarian who cares deeply about the effect government can have on people's lives. His father, a secular Jew, was a social worker and later became the deputy commissioner for public welfare for Philadelphia, (Someone had asked his father if he was disappointed that he was only deputy, and his father had said, "No, no, no," and turning to his son, he said, "Ted, you want to be number two, you don't want to be the number one.") His mother was Irish Catholic and had been a social worker and teacher. Ted is a devout Catholic himself. Now that he was finally moving from being the number two to out front, he told a reporter he was most concerned about "people with power taking advantage of the powerless."

Ted's association with Biden began in 1972, when he ran the voter-turnout organization for Biden's insurgent Senate campaign against a popular two-term Republican incumbent. The cause seemed hopeless, with polls before the election putting Biden thirty percentage points behind. Nevertheless, the upstart twenty-nine-year-old wound up winning narrowly. On the wall of his office, Ted kept a picture of the wild celebration that night and always said, "After that election, I'll never, ever, again believe that anything is impossible." Ted can tilt at windmills and genuinely believe he'll slay a giant. Because he once did.

But behind this optimism was a savvy realism. At the very beginning of our time together, Ted gave me what I thought was a great piece of advice: identify each staffer's strengths and use them; don't expect people to repair their weaknesses and don't assign them tasks they can't do well. I suspected that this was

something Ted had learned in part through his inter-
actions with Biden: Take advantage of Biden's
strengths, because after years of trying, you're never
going to change his weaknesses. Ted, along with Biden's
wife, Jill, sister Valerie, brother Jimmy, and sons (when
they became adults), tried to compensate for Biden's
weakness. They were the ones who exuded personal
warmth towards staffers. They were the ones who
called and stroked Biden's big campaign contributors
and fundraisers. They knew Biden would ignore every
task he didn't want to do and every person he didn't
want to deal with. So they filled in for him. Seen in a
positive light, they were using their strengths to com-
plement Biden's; in a negative light, they were system-
atically enabling his weaknesses and worst habits.

Ted and I made an interesting pair. Both of us were
insulated from the usual pressures of Washington. He
didn't have to raise a single dollar to get to the Senate
or in the two years he spent there. For my part, I was
older than most staffers and had already made my lucre
from lobbying. So I too felt immune to Wall Street's
power and the social and cultural glue that coats the
corridors of the Washington Establishment.

Ted was an engineer by training who also had an
MBA from the Wharton School at the University of
Pennsylvania and had worked in finance for the
DuPont Company. After graduating from Alabama, I
earned an MBA in finance from the University of
Chicago and then spent four years working for Wall
Street firms, first for Smith Barney and then for E. F.

Hutton. I later went to Stanford Law School before working in the Clinton White House Counsel's office. Ted had been investing for fifty years, I for twenty. Ted and I both saw ourselves as finance-savvy, even though we were in politics. For this reason, we thought very much alike and hit it off well.

Ted and I also had differences. One of them, I believe, reveals the deference that politicians—many of whom are extraordinary people whose breadth and depth of knowledge are often limited by the time drain of perpetual campaigning—show when dealing with hard-to-understand financial and economic issues and those who have mastered them. In October 2008, with the presidential election still roughly a month away, Ted and Mark Gitenstein (Ted's co-chair of the Biden transition team) came back from an Obama-Biden pre-transition meeting audibly excited that Bob Rubin, the former Clinton treasury secretary, might return to serve as Obama's. Ted and Mark were downright giddy. I wasn't. Maybe because of my experience in Costa Rica, I was stunned about what Rubin's excitedly anticipated return said about the Obama team. I feared it meant Wall Street in the White House. I feared that the people of this country would see right off the bat that one of Wall Street's own would ensure a bank-friendly approach to economic policy and that no banker would be held accountable.

Incredulous, I asked Ted: "Don't you realize that half the country wants to tar and feather Bob Rubin?" The *New York Times*, among others, had already reported on the extravagant compensation Citigroup had paid Rubin while he, ostensibly, had remained blind to the raft of rotten subprime mortgage products Citi had flogged to unsuspecting customers. Citi was, at that very moment, negotiating with the Bush economic team (with input from Obama advisors) to obtain a massive taxpayer bailout. And the Obama-Biden team thought Rubin deserved a promotion?

Even more stinging to me, as a fox-lobbyist, was seeing the foxes get free rein in the Obama henhouse. Ted and I watched closely, my disappointment growing and his optimism wavering. Michael Froman, Rubin's chief of staff in the Clinton Treasury Department, was a managing director at Citigroup while serving as the personnel director for the Obama pre-transition and transition. And whom did Froman bring in to help him with the job of picking top appointees for the Obama administration? James Rubin, the son of Bob Rubin.

Tim Geithner, then the president of the New York Federal Reserve Bank, was also a Rubin protégé. In late November 2008, Geithner would help pave the way for the Citigroup bailout, one of the first acts of the Obama transition. This happened while Froman was in a key position to influence Geithner's eventual appointment as treasury secretary. Froman would later trouser a $2.25 million bonus from Citigroup before departing to serve in the Obama administration.

Larry Summers, named director of the National Economic Council, had worked for Rubin at Treasury before succeeding him as secretary. He'd made more than $5.2 million in 2008 alone as a managing director of the hedge fund D. E. Shaw, and pocketed an additional $2.7 million in speaking fees from several future bailout recipients, including Goldman Sachs and Citi. At Treasury, Geithner's aide Gene Sperling earned $887,727 from Goldman Sachs in 2008 for performing the service of "advice on charitable giving." Geithner's future chief of staff, Mark Patterson, was a full-time lobbyist for Goldman Sachs (which raises the question of what was meant when we lobbyists were banned from serving).

It's no wonder that, if you ask almost any pollster, you'll be told that most Americans perceive no difference between Wall Street and Washington. Both are populated by power elites. Both pursue interests that differ dramatically from the national interest. One group, determined to make as much money as possible, misleads investors and, after a devastating financial crisis, asks taxpayers to foot the bill. The other group (regardless of political party) primarily courts campaign contributions from the wealthy and powerful, and, for the most part, plots long-term plans for attaining wealth and comfort in the private sector. Once absorbed by DC, members of Washington's Permanent Class serve as Wall Street's handmaidens: When they're in government they hire Wall Street alums for powerful government positions (after which the alums go back to Wall Street and make further millions). When they're not in government, they're working on Wall Street's payroll.

Unfortunately for America, Obama and Biden (who pledged in his 1972 campaign never to own a stock or a bond) were both financially illiterate. In the presidential debates, Obama did a fair impersonation of someone who had grasped the elements of the crisis (far better than John McCain). Ted told me the Obama internal polling showed that voters believed strongly Obama had bested McCain in the debates on the issue of how to grapple with the financial crisis. It may not have been why he ran for president, but Obama won foremost because the American economy direly needed effective leadership in the White House.

Yet Obama wanted to outsource the job of restoring America's financial health to Bob Rubin. Then, when Obama belatedly realized Rubin was toxic, he turned exclusively to Rubin's disciples, either oblivious or fully cognizant that Rubin and Rubinites were behind much of the deregulation that helped make the financial crisis possible.

Ted, who later turned against Geithner and railed about regulatory conflicts of interest from the Senate floor, was slow on the uptake. In late 2008, he still thought Geithner was great and that Hank Paulson (Bush's Treasury secretary) was the disaster. "Ted, how can that be?" I would ask. Paulson, Geithner, and Ben Bernanke (the Federal Reserve chairman) had been attached at the hip for every decision during the crisis. The difference between Paulson and Geithner was that Rubin had sprinkled his magic dust on Geithner, so Obama and his team were all cross-eyed for him.

Why did Obama turn to Wall Street from the beginning? Ted, who had attended the early transition meetings with President-Elect Obama and Vice President-Elect Biden, explained it this way: "It was like a car had broken down, and we needed a mechanic." In my view, it was a disaster from the beginning, with no one in the Obama finance team to offer a different viewpoint. Obama essentially entrusted the repairing of the china shop to the bulls who'd helped ransack it.

Although I was going to be his closest advisor, Ted didn't consult me on the question of which Senate committees to join. He told Senate Majority Leader Harry Reid that he wanted to be on the same committees as Biden: Judiciary and Foreign Relations. They were the two he knew best. I would've steered him toward the Banking Committee; outside it, he'd risk being shut out of financial reform. We'd simply never get enough information or have significant leverage.

From my lobbying days, I knew how the Banking Committee operated: Staffers gave lobbyists information about bills being drafted or what one senator had said to another (especially irresistible were scoops on the views of Chairman Chris Dodd or the ranking Republican, Senator Richard Shelby). The lobbyists passed the information on to their clients in the banking or insurance or accounting industry. The clients then forwarded a summary to their trade association or the Financial Services Roundtable. Sometimes within an hour, the news would be e-mailed to the entire financial-services industry and all of its lobbyists.

With multiple leakers from the Banking Committee keeping K Street well informed, the banking world had complete transparency into bill drafting, while senators who didn't serve on the Banking Committee stayed mostly in the dark.

Ted had never witnessed this side of the action. I had. But he caught on fast. At this time, he and I were learning, like everyone else, about the causes of the financial crisis and possible solutions. Because I knew prosecutors had all the tools they needed to pursue various types of fraud, I initially saw the crisis primarily as a law-enforcement matter. Somewhere in all this mess were people and firms who had broken the law, whether in isolated transactions or mass malfeasance.

I was determined that Ted (and Biden) should push for the establishment of a Justice Department task force—a strike force, really, of bank regulatory agency investigators, FBI agents, and prosecutors—dedicated to uncovering any fraud that had engendered the financial crisis. Ted was as gung-ho as I was.

In our early planning sessions, we discussed what had brought on the crisis. We knew the prevailing narrative. In 1999, Congress had repealed the Glass-Steagall Act, which had separated investment from commercial banking activities. Clinton's economic team (including Rubin and Summers) had fought to ensure that derivatives would remain unregulated. We knew that policymakers had pushed banks and quasi-agencies like Fannie Mae and Freddie Mac to make housing affordable; that subprime mortgages were pooled and securitized; that the rating agencies blew it and gave these pools AAA ratings; and that banks were leveraging thirty- and fifty-to-one and buying up these soon-to-be-toxic assets. Credit default swaps were being written and traded to hedge these risks without any understanding of who was writing how much and without any regulation or oversight.

As Ted liked to say, Washington's decades-long infatuation with deregulation had pulled all the referees off the football field. Then, the executives trusted to act in the best interests of shareholders had convinced themselves, against all reason and instinct, that they could engineer risk out of the system. Despite the fancy equations from the quants, the executives knew (or should've known) that they were gambling with shareholders' money. Once executives and companies realized the problem, many buried their heads in the sand. In some cases, as we did in Iowa, they faked it until they were dead.

In Ted's and my view, when confidence had been so shaken, when so much wealth had been destroyed, all options should be on the table for finding how best to reestablish wealth creation, restore public confidence, and protect investor interests. We believed Congress needed to restore the "solid edifices and critical pillars of our economic system"—which had crumbled, as even Alan Greenspan had admitted—wisely, carefully, and urgently.

Ted would focus from the beginning on enforcing the rule of law on Wall Street and restoring investor

confidence in our financial markets, a crucial prereq-
uisite for America's future economic success. Along
with creating jobs, what else should be a higher priority
for America's political leaders?

2:

HUNTING FOR
FINANCIAL FRAUD

TED'S FIRST DAY in the Senate was January 16, 2009. Biden and fellow Delaware senator Tom Carper escorted Ted onto the Senate floor, where Vice President Dick Cheney (in one of his last official acts) swore him into office. For the rest of Ted's time in office, the official photograph of Ted's large family standing in the Old Senate Chamber—where the Senate met from 1810 to 1859—had a "Where's Waldo?" quality. Admiring visitors (mostly Democrats) almost always did a double take when they suddenly spotted Dick Cheney standing next to Ted, Biden, and Ted's wife, Lynne.

After Ted had been sworn in, I watched from the Senate gallery as Senator Carper made generous welcoming remarks about Ted. We had hundreds of people waiting for Ted at a reception, and I could tell he was trying to figure out how to leave. Ted told me later Biden grabbed his arm and said, "Ted, you can't leave while Senator Carper is speaking." So Ted listened to Senator Carper. Ted had never before spoken on the Senate floor, so Biden grabbed Ted again and whispered, "Ted, when he finishes, pick up the microphone, right here" on one of the desks in the back "and say something nice about Senator Carper." So Ted picked up the microphone and said some nice things about Senator Carper. Then Ted went to the party and everyone commented, "Boy, you really looked like you knew what you were doing on the Senate floor." Ted said, "Well, if you're going to be staffed, you might as well be staffed by a vice president."

Each time Ted did something as a senator for the first time, it was an emotional milestone. His first caucus lunch (held on Tuesdays) with the other Democratic senators. His first vote. His first floor speech. We all had lumps in our throats. For every Senate staffer, Ted was a kind of hero, the one who had made it. All those years he had waited in the wings, all those times he had stayed behind, while Biden had gone to the Senate floor, the hearing room, the TV interviews, were behind him.

In January, Senator Kaufman and I walked over to the Judiciary Committee hearing room for the first time. Once there, Ted mentioned his views on prosecuting Wall Street fraud to Bruce Cohen, chief counsel to the committee's Chairman, Pat Leahy (D-VT), and then to Leahy himself. The timing was perfect. Leahy and Senator Chuck Grassley (R-IA) had been working on a bill entitled the Fraud Enforcement and Recovery Act, known as FERA. FERA was designed to give $165 million in additional resources to investigators and prosecutors to target financial fraud in connection with the financial crisis. Leahy immediately asked Ted whether he wanted to join as the third coauthor, and so the legislation became a Leahy-Grassley-Kaufman bill. Maybe we would pass a bill with "Kaufman" on it, after all. And this was only our first day. We'd said to Delawareans: Ted will hit the ground running. He did.

Leahy scheduled a hearing—styled as "The Need for Increased Fraud Enforcement in the Wake of the Economic Downturn"—to demonstrate the need for the additional funds. The witnesses included John S. Pistole, deputy director of the Federal Bureau of Investigation, and Rita Glavin, acting assistant attorney general for the Criminal Division of the U.S. Department of Justice. It was one of Ted's first hearings as a senator, and we'd worked carefully on his opening statement, which he practiced out loud in his office. The staff also suggested questions for Ted to ask, but Ted was determined to wing it and only ask brief questions based on what he learned at the hearing. Privately he said he was determined not to bloviate for the cameras, as he'd seen so many other senators do over the decades, but instead actually use the hearing as a learning experience.

Biden, a former stutterer, used to go through a speech draft and draw a slash after each phrase where he wanted to pause and breathe. It helped him not to rush his delivery and to give the statement a more natural-sounding rhythm. Ted did the same thing, striking with his pen a bit nervously as he worked his way through the pages.

When we arrived at the hearing, Leahy and Grassley were the only senators there. Ted's place along the curved committee dais was at the end of the Democratic quarter-moon, and that's where his nameplate was resting. Leahy motioned for Ted to sit next to him, so I walked over and grabbed the nameplate and brought it over before taking my seat along the wall, just behind my new boss. Chairman Leahy, as a courtesy, let Senator Grassley speak first. Leahy, a former prosecutor himself, went next. He recalled the Savings and Loan crisis of the 1980s and early 1990s and how the Judiciary Committee had helped to "rebuild the Department of Justice's ability to enforce fraud laws" after that national fiasco. As for the current financial crisis, Leahy believed that lax supervision in the mortgage industry had created an atmosphere of "Hey, come on in, fraud is welcome," and that "Wall Street financiers" had contributed to the disaster. Looking squarely at the witnesses, he concluded by saying that if anyone involved in the crisis committed fraud, "I want to see them prosecuted, and I want to see them go to jail." Then it was Ted's turn.

Ted began: The behavior of Wall Street bankers, credit rating agencies, mortgage brokers, and others all over the country came together in a complicated "confluence of factors" that led to the financial crisis. "I just have one overriding question," Ted said, pausing for dramatic effect. "Was any of that behavior illegal?"

The answer, he knew, was complicated. "As Attorney General Eric Holder said at his swearing in ceremony, 'only by drilling down' into Wall Street actions can we get to the bottom of it." Ted wanted to ensure that Congress gave investigators and prosecutors all the resources they needed to determine—repeating his main question—"whether any behavior was illegal."

In her testimony, Acting Assistant Attorney General Glavin laid out an impressive array of activist adjectives: the financial crisis demanded an "aggressive" and "comprehensive" response by law enforcement, a "vigorous" effort. She assured the committee that the department understood, as the attorney general had said, that it "must reinvigorate" its capacity to investigate financial fraud.

Leahy elicited an important comparison from Deputy Director Pistole. After the S&L crisis, the FBI had had 1,000 agents and analysts working on twenty-seven strike forces to target criminal activity. At the time of this hearing, Pistole said, the FBI had only 240 agents targeting financial fraud. And the fraud potentially involved in the current financial crisis, Pistole said, "dwarfs" that of the S&L crisis. Pistole also reminded the committee that the FBI had warned Congress several years ago about the increase in mortgage fraud. Pistole quoted the testimony in 2004 of former FBI Assistant Director Chris Swecker before the House Financial Services Sub-Committee:

> If fraudulent practices become systemic within the mortgage industry and mortgage fraud is allowed to become unrestrained, it will ultimately

place financial institutions at risk and have adverse effects on the stock market.

What's transpired since then, Pistole said, has been far worse than Swecker had predicted.

What had happened in fraud law enforcement since the S&L crisis and since Swecker's prediction in 2004? Not only did the FBI have far fewer agents working on financial fraud, but, in the run-up to the disaster, the law enforcement and regulatory system had failed to heed clear FBI warnings that mortgage fraud could become epidemic.

When it was his turn to question, Kaufman stated the obvious: "Clearly there are not enough agents." He wanted to know why. After 9/11, Pistole said, more than two thousand agents had been shifted to counter terrorism, and so the number of agents dedicated to investigating financial fraud was only a "fraction" of the number it had taken successfully to investigate S&L crimes. I cringed. No one would say it out loud, but America's aggressive (and perhaps excessive) response to foreign-bred terrorism had left it vulnerable to a home-grown fraud attack.

Ted asked Pistole whether the FBI would assign more agents to fraud and how it intended to enhance its ability to investigate complex, sophisticated financial transactions. Pistole answered that a "cadre" of agents had "honed and refined" their ability to understand complex financial fraud in the Enron case. The FBI would build on this cadre by hiring and training new agents. But Enron was one company. The potentially fraudulent mortgages that Wall Street had bundled and resold as securities had pervaded the banking and insurance industry in the U.S. and abroad. The FBI's then-dedicated resources looked inadequate for the mountain of potential fraud that needed to be investigated. Pistole testified that the FBI had already opened more than 530 corporate fraud cases, "including thirty-eight corporate fraud and financial institution matters directly related to the current financial crisis." Thirty-eight directly-related cases sounded like a lot and gave us some comfort, although Pistole warned that "the increasing mortgage, corporate fraud, and financial institution failure case inventory is straining the FBI's limited white-collar-crime resources."

Ted next asked Acting Assistant Attorney General Glavin whether it mattered that some of the fraud may have occurred in the derivatives market, which was unregulated. Would that diminish a prosecutor's ability to bring a fraud case against derivatives transactions? Glavin said no. Under federal mail-and-wire fraud statutes, for example, if you tell a lie over the phone or through the mail, you're subject to criminal prosecution. That the market was unregulated shouldn't matter.

After the hearing, in Ted's view, Congress couldn't pass FERA soon enough. Most of the bill had already been written by the time he joined Leahy and Grassley, so, with Leahy's strong encouragement, Ted put himself at the head of sales.

First, we came up with a catchy theme: "People know that if they rob a bank, they'll go to jail. Bankers should know that if they rob people, they'll go to jail, too." He wrote an op-ed for the *Philadelphia Inquirer*, which the newspaper headlined "Punish All Who Caused Crash" and ran next to a cartoon of a fat banker behind bars. He went to the Senate floor and thundered that this is a test of whether we have two justice systems in this country. The *New York Times* ran a Kaufman piece about FERA, which ended with the words: "For the markets to flourish again, the American people must be confident that we indeed have one system of justice in this country—whether for Wall Street or Main Street."

One of my law school classmates, Carlos Watson, was cohosting a mid-morning show on MSNBC, so I asked him to invite Ted on. Ted was a natural and struck the tone of a sheriff: "If people on Wall Street broke the law, we need to throw 'em in jail." More political and business shows on cable TV started inviting him on air. Not long after, the wife of another freshman senator met Ted and said to her husband, "He just got here, and he's already on TV."

In every TV interview, opinion piece, and speech, Ted made it clear that FERA funds would be used to catch the big fish on Wall Street who'd committed fraud, not small-fry mortgage hucksters. FERA, Ted said, was about "fighting the fraud on Wall Street, specifically in the buying, bundling, and selling of mortgage-backed securities."

In early March 2009, all the freshman senators met with the Federal Reserve chairman and the Treasury secretary. Ted reported back that Bernanke and Geithner were very concerned. On March 2, AIG had reported it had recorded a $61 billion loss in the fourth quarter of 2008. The next day, Treasury had announced an additional $30 billion in assistance to AIG, on top of the $150 billion it had already extended. Ted and others were wondering, "How could AIG lose $61 billion?" Bernanke and Geithner simply didn't know who held the credit-default swaps. There were similar problems in England, in Iceland, and at the Bank of Scotland. Ted said: "It was like a friend of mine who has this oak tree out in front of his house, a gigantic tree, and the tree is surrounded by a driveway. The roots were coming up and knocking out the driveway. But when they tried to put a new driveway in, they didn't know *where* the roots went. The roots went *all over.* I think that's how Bernanke and Geithner felt." On March 9, a few days after that meeting, the stock market reached its post-crisis low, with the Dow at 6,547.

On April 27, the FERA bill sailed through the Senate (ninety-two to four). The House then passed a similar bill. Congress, on both sides of the aisle, wanted to appear tough on sophisticated financial crime. FERA wasn't solely about adding resources. It included a few legislative tweaks that would help prosecutors in future cases. It also established the Financial Crisis Inquiry Commission, which was tasked with examining the causes of the financial crisis. But the heart of FERA, and the reason Kaufman promoted it so passionately, was its promise of substantial new resources to fight financial crime—resources needed to counteract the post-9/11 neglect of financial fraud.

We were thrilled to have chalked up a major legislative victory so soon, and for Ted to have played a significant role. Ted was invited to stand behind the president at the White House bill-signing ceremony on May 20, 2009, a rare and perhaps unprecedented honor for a freshman senator who had been in office for only four months. We felt good. We'd come into government determined to do something about financial fraud. And we'd already helped pass a landmark bill.

After the signing ceremony, our press release said: "Today marks a turning point for American confidence in our financial system. Our law enforcement agents and prosecutors will soon have the resources and training they need to find, prosecute, and jail those who committed financial fraud. Those who illegally lined their pockets and left investors—and millions of Americans—with the devastating consequences, will pay the price."

We were naïve. The bloom started to come off the rose during the appropriations process, in which bills are passed to fund the spending amounts that prior legislation (like FERA) had only authorized. Although decades in Washington had taught Ted and me that authorization isn't necessarily followed by appropriation, we were shocked to find that the Appropriations

Committee wasn't about to appropriate an additional $165 million to the Justice Department. Those funds would have to come from somewhere else, and there was simply no will or apparent ability to find them.

By that time, we'd hired Geoff Moulton as Ted's chief counsel to the Judiciary Committee. Geoff had many years of experience as an assistant U.S. attorney in Philadelphia (for a time, he was Beau Biden's boss) and had clerked on the Supreme Court for Chief Justice William Rehnquist. Geoff is a brilliant, even-keeled attorney. He was Ted's representative to Senator Barbara Mikulski (D-MD), chair of the Appropriations Subcommittee for Commerce, Justice, and State Department budgets.

Geoff reported to Ted and me that he had argued calmly and repeatedly to the Mikulski staff that Congress had just responded to a national crisis—in a very high-profile way, with a signing ceremony with President Obama at the White House—by authorizing $165 million for additional investigators and prosecutors, who were urgently needed, and it would be unconscionable for the appropriators not to follow through. He even pointed out that Mikulski, who eventually had signed on as a FERA cosponsor, had trumpeted the $165 million in new resources in a press release of her own. Mikulski's staff berated him, with the practiced aggression that no doubt came from daily sessions against dozens of senatorial claims on the public trough. Geoff, who'd never before worked in Congress or politics, was shocked at how emphatically the Mikulski staff shut its ears. Indeed, they argued in effect that FERA was irrelevant to the Appropriations Committee's work. The investigation and prosecution of financial fraud would be funded at the level the Committee deemed appropriate, FERA be damned. There's no more than $30 million extra, they said, and that's it. Maybe they'd be able to find more in the next budgetary cycle, they said, but, for this year, $30 million would have to do.

Ted and I talked about whether we should go public, whether he should blow the whistle on Senator Mikulski and the appropriators for short-changing the needed law enforcement effort. We considered offering a floor amendment to the appropriations bill to force a vote that might shame Ted's colleagues into fully funding FERA. Ted was far out on a limb, having first promoted and then celebrated FERA as providing huge new resources. We decided to keep our mouths shut. It didn't seem to make sense to embarrass Senator Mikulski (and Leahy, since he couldn't or didn't do anything about it). What people say about Congress is true: You often decide to go along to get along.

3:

"PLEASE STAY INVOLVED IN POLITICS"

AS TED AND I WORKED to deliver financial reform and a broader anti-fraud effort, I often recalled episodes from my more than two decades in Washington. I tried to draw on my experience to help me understand what was happening around me. I remembered what Valerie Biden Owens, Joe's sister, told me the first time I met Ted: "Ted doesn't have to worry, because he's so close to Joe."

It took me years to grasp all the ramifications of that sentence. But it didn't take me long to realize that attaching oneself like a limpet to a powerful, influential figure was the name of the game in DC—or, rather, the beginning of the game. It's certainly where I started. It also took me years to understand that, if you weren't so close to Joe, you ought to be worried, because that meant something as well.

In February 1987, I moved to Washington to join the Biden for President campaign. I rented a room in Alexandria from a man who told me he'd worked for almost twenty years for the Potato Chip Trade

Association. (Or maybe it was the trade association for all snack foods.) I remember thinking, "There's a trade association for potato chips?" His living room was adorned with framed photographs of him with famous senators and members of Congress. It was my first encounter with a power wall.

I didn't know when I looked at the potato chip wall that I'd one day join the ranks of what I call Professional Democrats. Or that this should be a personal goal. Despite the photographic evidence, back then I didn't understand what possible connection could exist between snack foods and senators. And I didn't foresee how the political culture of profit and ambition would, twenty-three years later, affect Ted's and my crusade to bring Wall Street to something approximating justice. I see it all now because a decade after I went to Washington I, too, had become a highly ambitious Washington insider seeking personal gain while facilitating the status quo. In other words, I'd become a Professional Democrat, one of thousands who earn a lot of money in the private sector while positioning themselves for better jobs in future Democratic administrations.

Washington is a place where the door between the public sector and the private sector revolves every day. A lawyer at the SEC or Justice Department leaves to take a position at a Washington law firm; a Wall Street executive takes a position at the Treasury Department. The former will soon be defending the Wall Street executives his old colleagues are investigating; the latter will soon be preventing (or delaying or diluting) any government policy that Wall Street doesn't like.

Senior officials, by leveraging the relationships they've developed while in Washington, can make millions after they leave government. To name just one prominent example from each party, Rahm Emanuel, a senior advisor to President Clinton, made $16.2 million as a self-described "relationship banker" at the investment firm Wasserstein Perella in less than three years after leaving the Clinton White House. Former Republican Senator Phil Gramm of Texas has made untold millions at the investment banking firm UBS (his wife, Wendy, a former chairman of the Commodity Futures Trading Commission, exempted Enron from derivative-trading regulations and a short time later took a seat on Enron's board of directors). Even mid-level staffers, people you've never heard of, can cash in. I know because I did. I barely registered on the DC power scale, but I still managed to earn millions as a lobbyist.

Don't get me wrong. There are thousands of competent, dedicated, hard-working staffers and civil servants in Washington who never cash in. Many of them simply can't: Their rank—and thus their value—is too low. But if you work your way up and become a key government official—in Congress or the executive branch (whether in the Justice, State, Treasury, or even Agriculture Department)—you can start test-driving Porsches in your final weeks in office.

These are the characters who while in the private

sector play intermediary roles in fundraising between special interests and Democratic elected officials, who facilitate communication between the governing and power elites, and who generally find ways to help the Blue Team beat the Red Team. If the Blue Team wins, those who wear blue jerseys can better attain power and wealth over the short and long term and take higher positions during their next round in government service. The Red Team of Republicans—across Washington's line of scrimmage—is playing the same game.

If the Marine Corps's hierarchy of allegiance is unit, corps, country, God, then the hierarchy for a Professional Democrat is current firm, former-elected-official boss, the congressional Democratic leadership, and the president (if he or she is a Democrat). At least that was my experience, and my experience began with Joe Biden.

Ed Gillespie wrote in *Winning Right,* his memoir, that in Washington everyone is someone's guy. Ed was a self-professed Karl Rove guy, Haley Barbour guy, and Dick Armey guy. Ed believed it meant loyalty: the willingness to go to the mat for someone. More than that, however, branding oneself this way makes political, social, and business sense. It signals to others that you belong to an inner circle within the Washington power culture. Under this taxonomy, I was a Biden guy.

I met Joe Biden when I was in college, followed him from afar, joined his staff, used him as a platform for my career, and generally climbed as high in government and as profitably in the private sector as I could.

I did all of this using the experience, knowledge, and contacts I'd gained since the day I set my sights on attaining power with Biden in Washington. I played out the Biden string—and I might say the Biden camp played out the Jeff string—to the very end. Eventually, I made my way up to Mount Everest (briefing a president—Clinton, not Biden) and to the top of K-2 (becoming a millionaire lobbyist). One way or another, it's the career trajectory for thousands of young people who move each year to DC. It starts with heady idealism and ends neck-deep in the Washington swamp.

I met Biden in 1979 when he came to speak at the University of Alabama. I was the leader of the student organization that had invited him, so I introduced him. Biden started by saying, "I know you're all here tonight because you've heard what a great man I am." There were only a few titters in the crowd. "Yep," Biden continued, "I'm widely known as what they call 'presidential timber.'" Now people began to realize he was being self-deprecating. "Why, just earlier tonight, I spoke to a group of students who had put up a great big sign, 'Welcome Senator Biden.' And then when I walked under the sign I heard someone say 'That must be Senator Bidden.'" He had the crowd going.

Biden said he was aware this event was part of a class for credit and was glad that there were so many young people in the audience. There were also some older people, whom he addressed directly: "You think the younger generation doesn't have the guts you showed in World War II, the moral backbone of your generation?" Nearly shouting, he said: "Well, don't tell me that until first you acknowledge that this country stood back for years when Hitler rolled over Poland, rolled over France, and when America knew Hitler had begun killing Jews by the thousands. Even when we fought World War II, we left the Jews stranded to die. We knew about the concentration camps, and President Roosevelt chose not to bomb the railway lines leading to them."

His remarks were apropos of nothing but certainly got the crowd's attention. Later, in the car back to the airport, Biden told me: "If you hit 'em early in the speech with something they don't like, something they don't agree with, you'll gain credibility. After that you can agree with 'em 98 percent on everything else, but they'll remember you had the guts to confront them."

Turning to the real topic of his speech, the SALT II arms control treaty then pending before the Senate, Biden, who spoke without any notes, explained the contents of the treaty, why he felt it was important to our national security, and the views of the various factions in the Senate.

Then he turned to that day's news about the discovery of three thousand Soviet troops in Cuba. Biden, almost whispering, said: "Folks, I'm going to let you in on a little secret." He walked with the microphone in his hand into the crowd, motioning everyone to lean forward to hear his secret. Then he yelled, "Those troops have been in Cuba all along, and everyone knows it!" The crisis was a sham, Biden argued, manufactured by the hawks to kill SALT II. Ever since the Cuban missile crisis in 1962, the Soviets had had as many as forty thousand troops in Cuba and had been drawing them down all along. Yes, there were still three thousand infantry troops in Cuba. No matter whether they were instructors or combat troops, they had no assault capability, no helicopters or ships that could deliver them to our shores. Besides, how afraid are we of three thousand Soviets invading Florida or Puerto Rico?

Biden whispered, thundered, argued, and explained for ninety minutes. He walked among the crowd. Finally, while still talking, he sat on the edge of the stage, in front of the lectern. He closed, after a long pause, by saying: "And that, students, is the end of tonight's class." After two seconds of complete silence—which I can still remember, even feel, today—two hundred Alabamans broke into sustained applause. Since I was sitting in the front row, I stood up (still applauding) to prepare to walk toward Biden to thank him. Once I stood up clapping, others behind me began to stand up. Within twenty seconds or so, by rising to my feet I had inadvertently started a standing ovation. (It was my first lesson in the importance of having a shill in the crowd.)

Biden's performance had been masterful, and admirers surrounded him afterwards. I felt vindicated for having chosen Biden to launch the Alabama Political Union lecture series, which I had founded and which was clearly off to a strong start.

That night, a campus security guard drove Biden back to the Birmingham airport. I hopped into the backseat and went along. I could tell Biden was exhausted, but the security guard started asking him questions. Basic questions about politics, like what was the difference between a Democrat and Republican. I rolled my eyes, fearing Biden wanted to relax. Biden actually couldn't have been more gracious. He answered the questions thoughtfully and respectfully. Biden's responsiveness only elicited more questions, each of which Biden took as seriously as if he was on *Meet the Press*. I started to ask him questions, too. He was just as engaging with me, treating us more like delegates to a national convention than a security guard and a nineteen-year-old kid he'd probably never see again.

Not familiar with Biden's biography, I asked him why he commuted to Delaware every day. With great self-possession and calm, Biden told me the story of how in December 1972, just a month after he'd been elected to the Senate, the car in which his wife, two sons, and baby girl were driving to pick up a Christmas tree was hit by a truck. The security guard driver and I were speechless.

"My wife and baby girl were killed," Biden continued, "and my sons were badly injured. So I stayed with my sons at the hospital. I really didn't want to be a senator. Eventually I was sworn in at my son's bedside. I served, but I went home every night to be with my sons. And, over the years, Delaware just got used to having me home every day, so I really can't ever move to Washington."

I was deeply moved. I knew at that moment that I was hooked on Joe Biden. The combination of the best ninety-minute extemporaneous, substantive speech on arms control I'd ever hear in my life, his thoughtful answers to a curious security guard's questions about politics, and finally his personal tragedy, told as if he was talking to one of his close friends, set the hook deep inside me.

When we arrived at the airport, the driver got Biden's bags from the trunk. I wanted Biden to sign something, but all I had with me was a spiral notebook with me. He wrote on the back of it:

To Jeff and the APU,
Please stay involved in politics. We need you all.
                                  Joe Biden, USS 1979

I did for the next 31 years, with that piece of cardboard framed and hanging on the wall of wherever I lived. Sometimes I eyed it with disdain, sometimes with admiration. Ultimately, I saw it as my meal ticket and, in a very real way, it had led to my position on Ted's staff.

In my senior year at Alabama I applied to four top law schools and four top business schools. I asked Dennis Toner, the Biden staffer I'd met, for a letter of recommendation from Biden, who knew that I'd launched the APU and later brought to Tuscaloosa the

National Collegiate Assembly, where Biden also spoke. Dennis warned me that Biden "doesn't do this for just any student," but in my case, thankfully, he did. This was my first step toward becoming a Professional Democrat. I wanted payback for what I did for Biden— and I got it. It was a transaction that set the stage for everything that was to come before I went to war with Ted Kaufman against Wall Street. After I got the letter, I also asked Dennis for a job on Biden's staff. I hadn't accumulated enough chips for that. Dennis encouraged me to first see which graduate programs accepted me.

I ended up going to business school at the University of Chicago. *Time* magazine had recently run a cover story about the increasing popularity and value of an MBA. The cover image was of a student wearing a mortar board, the tassel of which dangled a wad of cash. When I arrived in Chicago, I didn't have a clear idea what investment banking was. Within six months, I'd decided that, if Wall Street didn't hire me, I was a failure. Everyone wanted to be a banker or a management consultant; the dream employers were Goldman Sachs, Salomon Brothers, and McKinsey. The consensus among students was that only losers took jobs at companies that actually made things, like IBM or Proctor & Gamble.

I studied hard, often staying at Regenstein library until it closed at midnight. To take a break, I'd go to the stacks where old periodicals were kept. I'd pull out *Time* magazines from the 1960s and read about JFK, his administration, his assassination, Bobby's rise to prominence, and MLK's and Bobby's assassinations. The way I divided my time in Regenstein was symptomatic of a division in me. Part of me was engaged in intense competition with my fellow students to land a job on Wall Street, but another part of me wanted to go to Washington, where JFK had been, and where I was sure Biden would one day be president.

In my second year at Chicago, I sent applications to top investment banks, but also wrote several letters to Biden asking for a job on his staff. I made the mistake of addressing them to Biden himself and not to Dennis. To the people who opened Biden's mail, I was just another supplicant, and they never bothered to reply. With no word from Biden, I took a job at Smith Barney. I worked for them for a year in New York—yes, I'd made it to Wall Street—and for a year in Chicago. Then I moved to Atlanta to take a job at E. F. Hutton.

After two years at E. F. Hutton, I'd been promoted to assistant vice president. I was twenty-seven, had four years' experience as an investment banker, and was making good money. I hadn't forgotten Biden. I knew that he'd eventually run for president, and I still wanted to be part of it—and to be on his team in the White House when he won. Biden seemed to have forgotten me. He, or rather his office, hadn't answered one of my letters in six years, and Dennis and I had fallen out of touch.

In late 1986, I finally got an entrée. I met John McEvoy, a Washington lobbyist for E. F. Hutton (I was already entering the belly of the beast), and told him about my dream of helping Biden become president. He put me in touch with his former wife, Liz Tankersley, who was Biden's legislative director. Liz introduced me to Tim Ridley, a Biden staffer who would soon become the campaign manager of his presidential campaign. Tim offered me a job on the campaign for $24,000 a year, about one-fifth of what I was making at Hutton. I took it.

A week later, Tim asked me, before I officially started on the campaign, to do him a favor and "qualify" Biden in Georgia. To qualify for federal matching funds, presidential candidates have to raise at least $250 apiece from at least twenty people per state in at least twenty states. It was one of the hardest things I'd ever done, but I didn't want to fail my first Biden assignment. I begged everyone I knew in Georgia to do me this favor and managed to raise the money. One of the people I asked was my college girlfriend, who was by then married and living in Georgia. She'd heard (third-hand, as it happens) that "Biden would sell his own grandmother to be president." I told her it sounded like a rumor started by a disgruntled former staffer. She stood her ground and refused to write a check.

Then, mysteriously, Tim stopped returning my calls. And no one on the campaign could tell me my start date. For several weeks, I wasn't sure whether I really had a job. Finally, after I'd moved from Atlanta to my parents' home in Huntsville, Tim called. "Can you be here on Monday?"

That Sunday, I met Tim for brunch at the Hawk & Dove, a Capitol Hill restaurant. Tim, while terrible at returning phone calls, proved to be a shrewd yet warm-hearted political operative who had already won two Senate challenger races. To my surprise, Tim said my job wouldn't be at Biden's DC campaign headquarters. He wanted me to work for Ted Kaufman at the campaign's Wilmington office. I'd done such a great job qualifying Biden in Georgia that they wanted to make me a fundraiser. I was a little annoyed. My imagination had been captured by Biden the bold, substantive, and charismatic speaker. In contrast, calling people and begging them for money sounded awful. But I wanted to be a good soldier. So I said to Tim: "Just tell me where to go."

The next morning I met another new campaign staffer, Don Schimanski, at the train station. Together we went to Biden's Senate office in Wilmington, where we met Biden's sister, Valerie Owens, who had chaired all of Biden's campaigns. She introduced us to our new boss, Ted, who drove us to the campaign headquarters, located in a vast, blue-carpeted empty retail space in a less-than-thriving strip mall outside of town. Don and I walked around and introduced ourselves. Dennis Toner, who was working at one of the island desks in the sea of blue, remembered me and greeted me warmly. At one long table sat six elderly women volunteers doing what I later called the stick-donut-squiggle. They were forging a sticklike J, a donut-shaped O, and squiggly E at the bottom of hundreds of campaign letters.

Ted wanted me to help build organizational systems that would ensure that the fundraising operation had a plan and procedures for executing the plan. So, under his direction, I wrote a fundraising manual that I soon called The Bible. It described an Amway-like incentive system of captains and sub-captains in which the captains would build a pyramid of fundraisers and would get credit for all the money raised by their sub-captains.

The Bible's First Commandment was that no one gets to see the candidate without contributing $1,000. No exceptions. The Second Commandment was that people give money because of the person who's asking, not the candidate. I'd learned this while qualifying Biden in Georgia. Do it for me, I'd say. The last thing that would work would be actually to convince someone that Biden had a chance. The Third Commandment was that the more a captain raised, the more people he or she brought in as sub-captains (and the more they raised), the more access a captain would get to Biden. I was in charge of keeping track of the captains and sub-captains, what they each raised, what levels they reached in the access-to-Biden hierarchy, and what rewards—from a lapel pin to dinner with Biden—they received.

The Bible worked. After Gary Hart dropped out of the race, Biden, from tiny Delaware, was second in fundraising only to Michael Dukakis, who could harness the powerful fundraising machinery of a sitting governor in a populous state. Biden was second in some polls in Iowa and New Hampshire, as well. It seemed like my White House dream had a fair chance of coming true.

One day that spring, Biden came to Wilmington. Wearing a light turtleneck and aviator shades, he walked through the door of the campaign office looking like the $3.5 million we'd so far raised for him. He knew all the old Delaware hands, people who'd been volunteering for him since his first miraculous win in 1972. He took the time to talk to most of them one-on-one. Ted told us to gather round for Biden, who didn't seem to remember me. He didn't say much. He told us that he was getting a positive response from the crowds in Iowa and New Hampshire and thanked us for our hard work. Then he turned and left. I could've trotted after Biden and said, "Remember me? I promised you six years ago that, if you ever ran for president, I'd be there. Well, here I am." But by then I'd gotten to know many of the other young staffers, all of whom had their own Biden story that had brought them there. I had no reason to feel special. So, like the others, I went right back to work.

Eventually, I earned the spurs to take on my own fundraising territory for Biden: Texas and a couple of other southern states. My first stop was Houston. Whom do you call when you parachute into a city and try to put together a $50,000 event for Biden (or any Democratic candidate)? Jews and trial lawyers. (A few years later, Senator Howell Heflin of Alabama would say this out loud, naming "Jews, labor unions, and trial lawyers" as the financial pillars of the Democratic Party.

Soon I learned to add Hollywood and Wall Street to
that list.) Texas wasn't renowned for its labor unions,
but we knew of a couple of trial lawyers who were
Biden fans, along with a doyenne of the Jewish community. I went to see them first, and they gave me the
names of others.

In my pitches to these wealthy people, I tried to
sound like a smooth Washington operator. I had already begun to fake sincerity. "Roger, for $50,000 I can
get you dinner with the senator at his house. For
$25,000 I can get you dinner with the senator, but not
at his house." It was all about the access to the candidate and the appearance of a relationship with him. Access, relationship: Already I was learning the key words
I would need to help me understand Washington and
what I would find there. Already, I was beginning to
see the realities that explain why Ted Kaufman and I
would later have such a difficult time fighting the Wall
Street-Washington nexus.

The trial lawyers came through. We'd soon have
enough to make it worthwhile for Biden to fly to
Houston for a thank-you event. My offer to let the Jewish doyenne host the dinner at her house backfired. She
told me if we reduced the donation to $500 a plate she
could fill her house with people. I said no. It would
take a thousand to buy access. She was irritated. Nevertheless, we got the $50,000, and it was time for
Biden, his wife Jill, two other staffers who traveled with
him, and me to fly to Houston. Ted told me to find
Biden on the airplane and give him a briefing book

about the event, tell him who'd done the most and whom to thank. I still hadn't talked to Biden in six years. I'd been with the campaign for two months now, worked long days, and put together a $50,000 fundraiser. I felt I'd earned a moment of the candidate's time. So I walked up the aisle to the first-class section where Biden and his wife were sitting. "Senator Biden, may I speak with you for a minute?" Barely glancing up he said: "Just gimme what you got." So I handed him the briefing materials and returned to the back of the plane. Access denied.

Then things got worse. The plane couldn't leave, first because the flight catering was late and then because of a mechanical issue. An hour elapsed, and we were still at the gate. I was frantic. Fifty people who had written $1,000 checks would be sitting waiting. I called the hosts in Houston to tell them about the delay, and we agreed to go forward with the event. Finally, the plane took off. When we arrived in Houston, the police were waiting on the tarmac to drive us straight to the event. We were still going to be nearly three hours late. I'd already grown increasingly anxious on the plane and now I could sense a disaster looming. When we got there, Biden and Jill waded into the crowd, and those who couldn't get to him came up to me. My head was pounding, and I was a nervous wreck. It felt like film vérité: faces passing in front of me, speaking a language I temporarily couldn't understand. All I could manage to mumble in response was to "ask Senator Biden, he's your guy."

And then Biden started speaking: "I know you've been here a long time so I'll be brief." I could see irate expressions on faces around the room. Their message was easy to guess: We waited this long for you, pal; you'd better not head for the door until we've had our fill.

Days later, back in Wilmington, a letter arrived from one of the Houston contributors, complaining about the event and particularly about me. "Biden's staff guy was awful. He was rude and clueless." Ted laid the letter on my desk and never said a word about it then or later. In two months I'd gone from swearing I'd treat each Biden supporter like a precious jewel to pissing people off.

The payoff line of every Biden speech in 1987 was, "Just because they murdered our heroes doesn't mean the dream doesn't live still buried deep in our broken hearts." Allegedly, it had brought more than one Jefferson-Jackson Day dinner crowd to its feet, cheering wildly. It didn't speak to me. First, the imprecise use of the word "they" bothered me. Who was this "they" who had murdered our heroes? We're trying to beat the Republicans, not the assassins.

Biden's campaign felt derivative; he wasn't as bad as Gary Hart (who would stand with his hand in his suit pocket in imitation of JFK), but he was consciously trying to be a generational leader. As the pundits said, the Kennedys quoted the Greeks; Biden quoted the Kennedys. To be fair, the Kennedy legacy was tough to compete with.

That same summer, Lewis Powell retired from the Supreme Court, and President Reagan nominated Judge Robert Bork to take his place. It was a polarizing choice, since many believed that, if confirmed, Bork would create a majority that might overturn a number of previous Court decisions on matters relating to personal liberty, particularly *Roe v. Wade*. Senator Ted Kennedy made his infamous In-Robert-Bork's-America speech, which galvanized both Bork's opponents and supporters.

Biden, as chairman of the Judiciary Committee, would chair the confirmation hearings, and his performance was widely expected to be like a first primary election for him. If he performed well, his name recognition and status among Democratic primary voters might skyrocket. Biden threw himself into preparation, creating a council of legal advisors and constitutional scholars to brief him on the issues.

My own confidence was high because my life plan was on track. Biden would end up in the White House, and I'd have some kind of interesting role. The campaign was still a fairly small operation, and I realized that if Biden started winning primaries it would balloon overnight. Big Democratic operatives would join the team, pushing me further down the hierarchy. I didn't really care. The first thing we needed to do was win. My lust for power was beginning to take hold.

While dwelling on these happy thoughts, I took a weekend off in early September to go to Happy Valley for an Alabama-Penn State football game. As we drove up a winding two-lane road in Pennsylvania, I had the radio tuned to a local station. I heard a news report that presidential candidate Joe Biden had plagiarized a British labor politician. What?

That weekend in September 1987, Alabama beat Penn State, the defending national champion. My college buddies and I were elated as we left the stadium in Happy Valley. And though I was anxious to find out what was behind the news report we'd heard over the radio on the way there, I never imagined that within two weeks the Biden for President campaign would be over. It happened with dizzying speed.

Biden's peroration at campaign debates included a long quotation from a speech by Neil Kinnock, leader of the British Labor Party and the son of a Welsh coal miner. It asked the question why he was the first member of his family in a thousand generations to attend university. Had his ancestors—who worked twelve-hour shifts in the mines but read poetry at night—been too stupid? No, it was because he had a platform on which to stand.

Biden used the quotation in its entirety, including the strange reference to "a thousand generations" (was he suggesting there had been a Biden college graduate in Biblical times?), the British locution "go to university" (instead of the more American "attend university" or "go to college"), and the claim that his ancestors were coal miners (which of course they weren't). The quotation may have been ill-suited to Biden's biography, but he'd always unmistakably attributed it to

Kinnock. Except once—at a debate a few days earlier in Iowa. And someone, later revealed to be a Dukakis campaign advisor named John Sasso, created a video tape that placed Biden and Kinnock side-by-side saying the same words—and Biden not attributing them to Kinnock. Sasso knew perfectly well that it was a one-time lapse on Biden's part. Regardless, he wanted to cripple a rival campaign on the eve of Biden's big moment: the Bork hearings. So Sasso sent the tape to *NBC News* (which dismissed it as not newsworthy), the *Des Moines Register* (which printed a short story about it on page four), and the *New York Times* (which ran a devastating front-page story written by Maureen Dowd).

It got worse. That Sunday night, the national news led with snippets from Biden speeches side-by-side with speeches by Hubert Humphrey and RFK. Biden (or his speechwriters; many believe it was Pat Caddell) had lifted lines without attribution from his Democratic forebears. That night, at a cocktail party at Syracuse University, one of Biden's law professors mentioned that Biden had "failed to footnote properly" a long quotation from a source and had agreed to take an F in the class. This story somehow got passed along to the media. Biden now looked like a serial plagiarist. It seemed to undermine what he saw as his biggest strength: that he could move people, thanks to his skills as a public speaker.

The result of all this coverage was that every word Biden said publicly, or had said in the past, was being scrutinized for plagiarism or exaggeration. A particularly damaging example—indeed, the campaign's coup de grâce—was found in a four-month-old C-SPAN video that showed Biden speaking in a kitchen in a New Hampshire home. During the Q&A session, someone asked what Biden's grades had been like in law school. The correct answer was: not very good. It was a sore subject with Biden, and he snapped at the questioner: "I'll put my IQ up against yours any day." He then went on to claim that he'd graduated in the "top half" of his law class (he hadn't); attended law school on a full scholarship (he'd received a half scholarship based on financial need with some additional assistance based in part on academics); had three degrees (he has only two; he was counting his B.A. with a double major in history and political science as two degrees); and won an international moot-court competition (the competition had been in Toronto, so that claim, at least, was true). Eleanor Clift, at the time a reporter for *Newsweek*, found the video (she hadn't seen it when it originally ran) and wrote a story about it.

Of all Biden's screw-ups, this one concerned me most. Biden graduated seventy-sixth out of eighty-five—in other words, just outside the bottom tenth—at Syracuse University Law School. It seems fair to conclude that he found the curriculum harder—or that he worked less hard at mastering it—than all but a handful of his fellow students. There's no shame in that. Biden had passed the Delaware bar exam and had been a good trial lawyer. And I knew he could master complicated material. His highly detailed and extemporaneous talk about SALT II in Tuscaloosa proved that, and since then I'd seen him speak substantively and convincingly about a whole range of issues.

Biden had interpreted a dig about his law-school grades as an attack on his IQ. This suggested that he had an intellectual inferiority complex, and I can only conjecture that it's because he didn't have the accepted credentials of a brainiac: Biden wasn't a Harvard straight-A student, and Washington is filled with them. The telling part is that his sense of inadequacy compelled him to fabricate credentials that better suited the self-image of his intellectual abilities. The man I'd worshipped from afar was turning out to be all too human. Not fully happy with himself as he was, he tried—in little ways that had big consequences for his campaign—to be someone else.

The campaign flailed frantically, trying to stay afloat. Biden himself briefly stepped out of the Bork hearings to call an elderly African-American man who had been a cook at the diner that Biden had claimed he'd helped desegregate at a sit-in in the 1960s: "Do you remember? I was there. Can you tell people you remember me?" By then even Biden must have known it was over.

On the morning of September 23, 1987, Ted told me to call the fundraising captains across the country to let them know that Biden would withdraw that day at a 1:00 p.m. press conference. I dutifully called them all, trying to be as professional as possible, explaining that Biden felt he had no choice, and that by doing a great job chairing the Bork hearings he'd begin his rehabilitation. I thanked them each profusely and said we'd be in touch. About two minutes before the press conference, I called my parents. My mother answered. I couldn't say a word, but she knew who was calling. I finally managed to say, "Turn on the TV," and then broke down. While others listened to Biden's statement, I walked into the bathroom and wept.

Later that week, Biden came to the Wilmington headquarters. "I've never quit anything in my life," he said, "when people were looking." That was mildly amusing, but it didn't temper my feeling that my hero had been exposed as a phony. Biden—like Spiro Agnew, Earl Butz, and Alexander Haig before him—had entered the popular imagination not for his political achievements but for his gaffes.

Ted asked me whether I could stay in Delaware for a couple of months to help shut down the campaign. I said yes, remaining a loyal Biden soldier even after the general himself had retreated, hopefully to fight another day. To be honest, I didn't really have a better option. I'd walked away from investment banking, gone all in with Biden, and now, after Biden's ignominious exit, I had no idea what I was going to do next.

So I did what Ted asked. It was misery. And it was only exacerbated by my other unenviable task, which was to relive Biden's downfall in excruciating detail by cataloging all of the news articles and opinion pieces written about his controversies and decision to withdraw. The next election for Biden's Senate seat was in 1990, and that campaign team would need a database of the material from which potential opponents (and the media) would draw their barbs. There were hundreds of articles, at least one from almost every newspaper in the country. Many of them were brutal. Biden had sunk so low in the final days of his campaign that nothing, no aspect of his personality or his person, was out of bounds. Even Biden's hair plugs became the object of opinion pieces. They were seen as symbols of his cut-and-paste persona and as evidence that he was unfit for office: Could any man who felt the need to mask his bald spot by surgically moving tufts of hair be entrusted with the presidency?

During the time I was dismantling the campaign and archiving Biden's downfall, Ted offered me a job on Biden's Senate staff in Washington at a salary of $48,000 a year. I wasn't impressed. That's what an administrative assistant made at E. F. Hutton. Ted assured me that "by Senate staff standards, this is huge, it's positively munificent." And Biden was still my hero, albeit a tarnished one, and if he wasn't in the White House (yet), I'd serve him where he was: in the Senate. Moreover, Ted and I had developed a strong bond. He knew the value of an able lieutenant, and I liked working for him and knew he was Biden's closest advisor. I'd figured out that the best way for me to help Biden was to help Ted. That's what I did for the next twenty years.

Within days of my arrival, lobbyists started calling me and taking me to lunch. These meetings were helpful: I needed a quick primer on the issues before the committee, and the lobbyists knew them backwards and forwards. I had misgivings about their picking up the check all the time (this was well before Congress finally enacted a ban on all gifts). One lobbyist told me, "Jeff, Jesse Unruh said it best: If you can't eat their food, drink their liquor, and get up and vote against them in the morning, you don't belong in this business." I compromised by agreeing to go to lunch only at the Monocle, a restaurant that had been cited a few years before for health violations. The lobbyists always begged me to go somewhere nicer. I held my ground. It was the Monocle or nothing. I'd accept free food but only from a bad restaurant. How's that for ethics?

As my time in his office continued, one fact became clear: I just didn't hit it off with Biden. Only a handful ever made it into his inner circle (which is true for many successful politicians, whether for self-absorbed or simply cautious reasons). I simply wasn't one of the chosen.

As time passed, I tried to understand why Biden had appealed to me so much in the beginning and then how I saw him after the fact—after his campaign downfall and after working on his staff for a time. In Alabama, I'd watched him train his charisma beam on people of all ages and, as far as I could tell, win them all over. In Washington, he would do the same thing with complete strangers, especially if there was any hint that they might be from Delaware. Yet, behind the scenes, Biden acted like an egomaniacal autocrat and apparently was determined to manage his staff through fear. Like Napoleon, Biden had captured his personal Toulon at a very young age. In comparison, his tentative young staff must have seemed like an army of underachievers. I decided I'd stay until I could help him regain his professional balance and then move on to something else.

Ted invited me to sit in on meetings and get more involved in Biden's inner circle of advisors, most of whom had been with him for nearly two decades. My background was in banking and my campaign experience had been brief, so political strategy was new to me. I spent most of these strategy meetings soaking in what I heard and waiting for a brilliant idea to hit me. To be honest, I didn't contribute much. Indeed, I often had the impression we were quibbling about minor differences between nine equally fine different ways to skin a cat.

At a meeting in 1989, we were thinking up themes for drug-policy hearings that Biden could chair. Biden was trying to focus national attention on cocaine addiction, particularly on the devastating effects of crack cocaine in urban neighborhoods. Ron Klain, who had succeeded Mark Gitenstein as Biden's chief counsel, wanted to have Hollywood executives testify about the movies' impact on drug use. Ted proposed several ideas and then turned to me and asked, "Jeff what do you think?" I didn't have a single idea. Moreover, I found the whole exercise silly. We were thinking up ways for

Biden to get press attention so that when people think drug policy and law enforcement they think Biden. He'd already been holding a weekly drug-policy hearing for years now. In my mind, the focus was too much on designing hearings that would enhance Biden's brand image as tough on crime and too little on hearings that would help the Senate get the information it needed to write effective legislation. It was at this meeting that I decided to apply to law school.

I left the Biden staff in May 1991 to travel for a couple of months before starting at Stanford in late August. At my going-away party, I gave a little speech to Biden and the rest of the staff. It included an anecdote about how I'd provided briefing material and talking points to Biden for a Senate floor speech just days ago. I said what a powerful, effective speech it had been and that it left me just as impressed with Biden as the first time I'd heard him speak almost fifteen years ago in Tuscaloosa. The only difference, I said, was that those were my talking points on the lectern he was ignoring. The staff laughed knowingly. We'd all had the experience of slaving over speech texts and talking points that Biden chose not to use, preferring instead to extemporize. My punch line didn't even elicit a smile from Biden. In all my conversations with him, I don't think he ever laughed at one of my jokes.

4:

WHERE ARE THE CASES?

AS 2009 WORE ON, despite the thirty-eight investigations we'd been told about, indictments against Wall Street executives and directors failed to materialize. It wasn't because of the funding shortfall. The Justice Department, FBI, and SEC were each going forward with their investigations, coordinating with each other informally and through a variety of interagency task forces. Like us, these agencies knew not to cross Senator Mikulski; they, too, played long-term strategies to get more funding. In the meantime, they worked with the resources they had.

From the beginning, Ted and I feared that the Obama administration leadership might tend to let Wall Street off the hook so as not to impede the economic recovery. Geoff, Ted's chief counsel on Judiciary, kept assuring us that every prosecutor would love to bag a big Wall Street defendant. There was no shortage of dedication and enthusiasm on the front lines. But would front-line prosecutors get the time and investigative resources they needed to "drill down" into Wall

Street, as Attorney General Holder had put it? The situation was further complicated by a recent jury verdict. In the fall of 2008, the U.S. Attorney's Office for the Eastern District of New York had lost a case against two Bear Stearns defendants who had been charged with securities fraud for lying to investors about the strength of their hedge fund, which was filled with toxic mortgage-backed securities. The jury's swift not-guilty verdict in the first criminal case stemming from the financial crisis may have had a chilling effect on line prosecutors and their superiors.

In the Enron case, a well-staffed team of investigators and prosecutors had gained convictions of CEO Ken Lay and CFO Jeffrey Skilling. But, in the wake of the financial crisis, the Justice Department didn't form task forces to investigate AIG, Lehman Brothers, Countrywide Financial, Washington Mutual, Goldman Sachs, Citigroup, or the other potential targets. Moreover, two sources were telling me that Christine Varney, the assistant attorney general for the Antitrust Division, was complaining to friends that Rahm Emanuel, then White House chief of staff, had sent her a message: in effect, throttle back on antitrust enforcement, because the top priority is economic recovery. I was concerned that Attorney General Holder had gotten the same message about investigating Wall Street crime.

William Black, an economics and law professor at University of Missouri at Kansas City who played a key role in the prosecutions that followed the S&L crisis, had predicted this problem: the fear that targeting banks could cause them to collapse and further damage the economy. "There are excuses," he said to the press, "not to prosecute corporations. People are scared to death of the pushback, politically, if you cause a company to fail. As long as we have that kind of attitude, you will have no deterrence. I fear the new administration has not learned that lesson at all." Arthur Andersen, once one of the big five accounting firms, had voluntarily closed after being found guilty of criminal charges related to its auditing of Enron (the Supreme Court subsequently overturned the conviction).

Yet Eric Holder had pledged to make targeting Wall Street a priority. After being sworn in by Biden, Holder told reporters: "We're not going to go on any witch hunts, but to the extent that what this nation is facing is the result of fraud and misconduct, we'll find it and we'll hold people accountable." And that was the point: people were responsible for the financial crisis and people can be prosecuted. Prosecutions need not target the firms that we'd already learned were too big to fail (and, by the same theory, might be too big to prosecute).

Holder had left a lucrative law practice at Covington & Burling, my old firm, where he'd defended corporate clients in criminal probes, to take over a department that had already seen its record on financial crimes come under attack. And he picked Lanny Breuer, a fellow Covington partner, to be assistant attorney general for the Criminal Division. I didn't know which clients Holder and Breuer had represented at

Covington, but I knew it was as white-shoe as any law firm gets, and that it had dozens of banks and financial services firms as clients. Were these the right guys to ensure a get-tough approach at a department that was already falling behind in investigating the financial crisis?

Ted and I were determined to push the Justice Department and SEC as hard as we could. In those early months, we took Justice Department and SEC leaders at their word when they said, publicly and privately, that they were making these cases a priority, that it would take time to develop them because of their complexity, and that they needed additional resources from Congress to do the job more effectively. It's natural to want to trust law-enforcement officials. And natural for Congress to support them and then stand back and let them do their jobs.

But months crept by. And still nothing happened.

Ted decided to ask Chairman Leahy if he could chair an oversight hearing of FERA. Oversight of the executive branch is one of Congress's most important responsibilities, but something it always seems to do a day late. Ted wanted to prove it could be done in real time, on this and other brewing financial issues. He wanted to make certain the Justice Department was using the FERA money (even if only $30 million) and other resources effectively. The purpose of the hearing would be to ensure that Justice, the FBI, and the SEC were making the targeting of high-level fraud a top priority. That they would plan, staff, fund, and direct a thorough, probing investigation of each of the primary potential defendants.

In the summer of 2009, we asked Lanny Breuer, by then confirmed by the Senate as the new assistant attorney general for the Criminal Division, for a meeting. It was September before Breuer and his top team of fraud-enforcement advisors could see us. When we finally had the meeting, we sat around the conference table in Ted's suite of Senate offices. Ted started by saying he appreciated all the effort that he knew was under way, but that Chairman Leahy had asked him to chair an oversight hearing, which would create a public forum for learning about the strategy and direction of the Justice Department's and FBI's investigative work.

This was news to Breuer and the other Justice Department lawyers, and it certainly got their attention. In the chitchat prior to the meeting, Breuer had mentioned that he'd done a series of speeches to the white-collar bar and that he was going to Romania (where former Biden staffer Mark Gitenstein serves as ambassador) to give a speech. I remember wondering: "What is he doing spending all his time on a speech tour?"

Breuer proceeded to tell Ted about how few resources his division had and that he'd been struggling even to get laptops for his lawyers. We winced about the underfunding ($30 million instead of $165 million) and said we felt badly about it. And the subtext of the meeting was that the U.S. attorneys across the country in reality report to the deputy attorney general, not to Breuer or to any of the other assistant attorneys general, and as a result Breuer wasn't able to direct their operations.

At one point in the meeting, Breuer said the department was dependent on the "pipeline" to bring forward cases. That's when I lost my temper. "Lanny, you need to go down into your pipeline and make sure the FBI and U.S. attorney's offices are making this a top priority. Organize and shake your pipeline hard and get it to bring you cases. Don't just sit back and wait." I also couldn't resist invoking our mutual history in the White House Counsel's office and even exhorting him to emulate the tactics of our former antagonist. "You need to be like Ken Starr. You need to target some of these guys like they were drug kingpins, just like Starr targeted Clinton, and squeeze every junior person around them until you can get one to flip and give evidence against the senior people." I also passed on William Black's advice: that the bank regulatory agencies needed to help the FBI by developing background materials for criminal referrals. It was only after Congress rattled these agencies into action after the S&L crisis that they sent referrals with summaries and exhibits as roadmaps for further FBI investigation. These referrals led to hundreds of successful prosecutions.

I could tell from the expressions of Breuer and his team that nothing like that was happening (indeed, they admitted that, so far in 2009, the bank regulatory agencies hadn't provided a single referral). It was eight months since Holder had said he'd make fighting financial fraud a top priority, and the department heads were still swanning around giving speeches and fighting for laptops for their staff. Ted, Geoff, and I had the impression the department wasn't on top of the situation. Valuable time was slipping away, and the trail was only going to get colder.

The hearing was scheduled for December 2009. Before that, we also asked the FBI for a meeting. When Kevin Perkins, assistant director of the FBI's Finance Division, came to our conference room, he gave a presentation about the matrix the Bureau was using to track evidence of mortgage fraud. It was impressive, but Ted quickly seized on the fact that the investigation was targeted exclusively on small-fry mortgage brokers and bankers; we heard nothing about investigations of the higher-level securitizations by major Wall Street firms.

About a month later, the Justice Department announced the formation of a Financial Fraud Enforcement Task Force (FFETF). Ted had heard that the idea of a task force had been dying a slow death owing to interagency wrangling and that only the prospect of a public hearing had moved it back on to the administration's agenda. We were told by one U.S. attorney's office that the department had just asked them for the first time whether they were working on any financial fraud cases. The anecdotal evidence we had indicated that central Justice wasn't leading the effort and that U.S. attorneys around the country were to do as they thought best. Although I feared that FFETF was merely window dressing to give Justice something to show and tell at the Kaufman hearing, I hoped it would change the current decentralized—and desultory—approach to investigating financial fraud.

Several days before the hearing, Geoff and I talked by phone to Rob Khuzami (the SEC's enforcement director) and two of his lieutenants. We didn't want to surprise Khuzami at the hearing, so we gave him a preview of Ted's opening statement and most of his questions. Khuzami was impressive. He'd worked at the U.S. attorney's office in the Southern District of New York, where he had prosecuted Omar Abdel-Rahman for the 1993 World Trade Center bombing. He'd left to become general counsel of Deutsche Bank, so he knew a lot about Wall Street transactions. Khuzami laid out his team's plan for pursuing fraud against a matrix of firms, transactions, and types of securities. Geoff and I thought he was thoughtful, organized, and methodical. We also hoped that despite his Wall Street background he was determined to be tough on financial fraud.

At the December 2009 hearing, the three witnesses—Breuer, Khuzami, and Perkins—said all the right things. Don't worry. We're on the case. These are complex financial frauds committed by sophisticated actors. It takes time and patience to develop these cases. We're reviewing the facts and the evidence. We'll bring criminal or civil actions where the facts take us. Stay tuned.

At the time, we believed them. Unraveling sophisticated financial fraud is an enormously complicated and resource-intensive undertaking, because of the nature of both the conduct and the perpetrators. Khuzami put it this way during the hearing:

> White-collar area cases, I think, are distinguishable from terrorism or drug crimes, for the primary reason that, often, people are plotting their defense at the same time they're committing their crime. They are smart people who understand that they are crossing the line, and so they are papering the record or having veiled or coded conversations that make it difficult to establish a wrongdoing.

In other words, Wall Street criminals not only possess enormous resources, they're also sophisticated enough to cover their tracks as they go along, often with the help, perhaps unwitting, of their lawyers and accountants. After the hearing, we were confident that we had gotten Justice's and the FBI's attention and that our law enforcement agencies were doing their best.

Still, nothing happened.

Of course we wanted to know why. But our oversight was primarily about ensuring that law-enforcement agencies had a clear strategy, were coordinating with each other, and didn't face systemic obstacles that might hamper their effort. It was difficult to find out what was happening on an operational level because we couldn't ask the agencies about evidence in any particular case. Moreover, the controversy over the Bush administration's firing of seven U.S. attorneys (including allegations that Senator Pete Domenici [R-NM] had inappropriately made a phone call to the U.S. attorney in his state about a pending investigation), was still fresh in everyone's mind. We knew that demanding answers about particular cases, however well-intentioned we were, would be a mistake. Ted was determined to conduct meaningful oversight, without stepping over the line.

5:

LEHMAN AND WAMU

IN MID-MARCH 2010, the bankruptcy examiner for Lehman Brothers Holdings Inc. released a twenty-two-hundred-page report about the demise of the firm. The report, which included eye-opening details about Lehman's accounting practices, put in sharp relief what we, and many others, had suspected all along: that fraud and potentially criminal conduct were at the heart of the financial crisis. This was the first case where we were able to see the facts as developed by a competent and independent fact-finder, unlike the shrouded investigations under way at the Justice Department and SEC (even in our private meetings with the Justice Department, FBI, and SEC, we still hadn't learned any details about specific cases).

The bankruptcy examiner's report was devastatingly unequivocal. It stated clearly that Lehman had cooked its books, hiding $50 billion in toxic assets by temporarily shifting them off its balance sheet in time to produce rosier quarterly reports. The bankruptcy examiner called Lehman's financial statements "materially misleading" and said its executives had engaged in "actionable balance sheet manipulation."

Lehman Brothers may have gone under, but the people responsible for this fraud are still around. Why aren't these people being prosecuted and, if found guilty by a jury, going to jail?

After the release of the bankruptcy report, I worked all weekend on a speech for Ted entitled "Restoring the Rule of Law to Wall Street." On Monday, Geoff and Jane Woodfin, Ted's legislative director, helped me polish it. The next day, Ted was the first on the Senate floor to speak. He blasted Lehman, Wall Street's Wild West attitude, the colossal failures of accountants and lawyers who misunderstood or disregarded their role as gatekeepers, and the inaction of government prosecutors. "We must concentrate law enforcement and regulatory resources on restoring the rule of law to Wall Street. We must treat financial crimes with the same gravity as other crimes, because the price of inaction and a failure to deter future misconduct is enormous."

One unexpected benefit of Scott Brown's election to the Senate in early 2010 to fill Ted Kennedy's seat was that it opened a Democratic seat, which Ted filled, on the Permanent Subcommittee on Investigations (PSI), which Senator Carl Levin (D-MI) chairs. The PSI has subpoena power and a broad mandate, wielded by its Chairman, to investigate corruption. Levin and his staff had been investigating the financial crisis for more than a year, and he'd decided to accelerate the dates for a series of hearings on Washington Mutual

(WaMu), the Office of Thrift Supervision (OTS), credit-rating agencies, and Goldman Sachs. The hearings would illuminate the chain of wrongdoing from the mortgage-origination level, to the failure of bank regulators and credit-rating agencies, to the securitization and packaging of subprime mortgages by Wall Street banks.

The first three hearings (on WaMu, OTS, and the credit-rating agencies) received far less attention than the final hearing on Goldman Sachs, but they were devastating. Evidence gathered by the subcommittee demonstrated that WaMu executives tolerated, and possibly encouraged, widespread fraud as part of an effort to dramatically expand loan volume. Approximately 90 percent of WaMu's home equity loans were so-called "stated income" loans (known more glibly and more accurately as "liar's loans"), which allowed borrowers to state their income on the loan application without providing any supporting documentation. As Treasury Department Inspector General Eric Thorson said at the hearing, WaMu's high percentage of stated income loans created a "target rich environment" for fraud.

An internal review of a WaMu loan office in Southern California revealed that 83 percent of its loans contained instances of confirmed fraud; in another office, the figure was 58 percent. And what did WaMu management do when it became clear that fraud rates were rising as housing prices began to fall? Rather than curb its reckless practices, it decided to try to sell a higher proportion of these risky, fraud-tainted mortgages into the secondary market, thereby locking in a profit for itself as it spread the contagion into the capital markets.

The second hearing showed that OTS had failed abjectly to regulate WaMu and to protect the public from the consequences of WaMu's excessive risk-taking and toleration of widespread fraud. Although WaMu accounted for 25 percent of OTS's regulatory portfolio, OTS adopted a laissez-faire approach. OTS's front-line bank examiners had identified the high prevalence of fraud and weak internal controls at WaMu, yet the OTS leadership did virtually nothing to address the situation. In fact, OTS advocated for WaMu with other regulators and, in 2007 and 2008, had actively thwarted an investigation of WaMu by the Federal Deposit Insurance Corporation (FDIC). The explanation for OTS's complete abdication of regulatory responsibility may be that it was dependent on WaMu's user fees for 12–15 percent of its budget. The hearing exposed the spectacle of a regulator competing for business (WaMu and other banks could choose whether its primary regulator would be OTS or the FDIC) by currying favor with the very entity it was supposed to regulate, just so it wouldn't lose the revenue stream to another regulator. This was more than the perhaps inevitable coziness that comes from long interaction. This was a system structured to make regulatory capture inevitable.

At the hearings, Treasury Inspector General Thorson

said he didn't know whether regulators' hesitation to take any action was "because they get too close [to the banks] after so many years or [because] they're just hesitant or maybe the amount of fees enters into it. . . . But whatever it is, this is not unique to WaMu and it is not unique to OTS."

After the hearings, Ted went to the Senate floor and praised Levin's work, comparing it to the Pecora Commission of the 1930s, which had galvanized Congress to pass major Depression-era reforms. As for Ted and me, we were both becoming convinced that there was fraud for the government to prosecute.

Where were the Justice Department and the SEC? Two thorough investigations—Lehman by the bankruptcy examiner, WaMu by the PSI—had uncovered what certainly looked like fraud. The PSI and bankruptcy-examiner reports were strong indications that when competent, motivated, and well-led investigators look at what took place in the financial crisis, they find evidence of fraud. With no indication that the prosecution of either fraud was imminent, Ted and I were now deeply concerned.

Why weren't we seeing any cases? There were at least three possibilities. First, it was too soon. The investigation of complex financial fraud is a long process; in time, the cases would come (as it turns out, they never did). Second, there was no provable criminal conduct. The Justice Department and the SEC had turned over every rock, considered every piece of evidence, and concluded that mass delusion, not fraud, had caused the crisis. In light of the Lehman bankruptcy report and the PSI hearings (and the absence of real commitment by the Justice Department), that possibility was easy to dismiss. Third, the failure of the government to take a timely, targeted, all-in approach to the problem had condemned it to failure. When investigating complex fraud perpetrated by sophisticated, well-advised actors able to bury disclosures in mountains of paper, anything less than timely and full commitment won't be enough. Increasingly, it looked like this third possibility was the sad answer to our question.

6:

WHAT HAD GONE WRONG?

FINALLY, IN APRIL 2010, the SEC announced that it had a case. It filed charges against Goldman Sachs for the Abacus collateralized debt obligation. The case alleged that Goldman had failed to disclose the involvement of a hedge fund (which intended to short, or bet against, the security) in the portfolio selection process. This news gave us hope that the SEC was back on the job and that even the most powerful on Wall Street would be held accountable. In Ted's eyes, Khuzami, who oversaw the case against Goldman, was a hero. Until the day he left office, Ted would continue to encourage and defend Khuzami.

When the SEC settled with Goldman that summer for a record $550 million, many thought Goldman had gotten off easy. Ted, however, rushed to Khuzami's defense in a posting on the *New York Times* DealBook. He wrote that the fine is evidence the SEC is "back on the beat." Khuzami had taken on Goldman Sachs, "the ultimate in a sophisticated, powerful defendant with access to armies of the best lawyers and deepest pockets to defend any case. . . . Whatever you might think about the deal, no one should believe Goldman walked away with anything less than a very bloody nose."

Ted went further out on a limb, personally vouching that the SEC and Justice Department were fully invigorated, well led, motivated, and determined to root out financial fraud associated with the financial crisis, even among the highest paid and most influential. We so wanted to believe that they were.

During the next four months, no noteworthy cases emerged, only settlements (for trifling sums) engineered by the SEC. The settlements angered a number of federal judges, who lambasted the SEC for letting individuals off the hook and failing to achieve adequate deterrence. When I later raised the judges' objections privately with Khuzami, he said to Ted and me: "I'm not losing any sleep over them." I retorted: "Why not? It seems to me they've put the key question squarely on the table: Is the SEC achieving the level of accountability and deterrence that the facts demand?" Khuzami merely glared at me and went back to talking to Ted.

What had gone wrong? When Ray Lohier (now a judge on the Second Circuit, U.S. Court of Appeals, but during 2008–09 the assistant U.S. attorney in the Southern District of New York in charge of the securities-fraud division) made his courtesy visit to members of the Judiciary Committee in the spring of 2010, he met with Ted and me. Ted asked him, "What is your current top priority?" Lohier responded, "Cyber crime." Our jaws dropped. For the last eighteen months, we'd been vociferously prodding the Justice Department to target high-level Wall Street fraud. But the message still hadn't gotten through to the man who had held the key position. Hacking into a Wall Street bank's computers to steal money is a crime. It should be investigated and prosecuted. But what about the banks' potentially fraudulent actions that harmed so much of the rest of the country?

The truth is, the Justice Department never made investigating these actions a high priority. It never formed strike forces of investigators and lawyers that had sufficient resources and backing to doggedly pursue the obvious potential wrongdoers as long as it took to bring a fraud case. This view was substantiated by subsequent reporting by George Packer at the *New Yorker* and Gretchen Morgenson and Louise Story at the *New York Times*. Indeed, it wasn't long before the Justice Department leaked to the media that it wasn't going to bring indictments against Joseph Cassano, a former top executive at AIG, or Angelo Mozilo, former chief of Countrywide. Why so soon and so publicly? I knew of people who'd been harassed by prosecutors for years and were never told they were off the hook. So I was surprised that department lawyers had swiftly announced that central players in the financial crisis were in the clear.

At the time, the U.S. Attorney's office for the Southern District of New York (SDNY) was successfully prosecuting a number of big insider-trading cases. Though laudable, these cases had nothing to do with the financial crisis. Wiretaps had produced ample and damning evidence of insider trading, so perhaps the SDNY had decided to focus on this productive avenue of prosecution. But I suspect the decision stemmed, at least in part, from the fact that the SDNY never felt it had the full backing of Justice Department leadership to devote massive resources and time against major Wall Street actors in the financial crisis. Indeed, even though the SDNY is by far the best-equipped U.S. attorney's office for conducting sophisticated securities-fraud investigations, the department had spread responsibility for these investigations to other smaller and less-experienced offices. What's more, Attorney General Holder also gave the SDNY high-profile, resource-draining terrorism cases like the prosecution of Khalid Sheikh Mohammed, the mastermind of the 9/11 plot (this decision unleashed a firestorm of criticism, and Holder, seventeen months later, reversed it). This mattered, I believed, both because of the resource drain (subsequently alleviated) and because of the message it sent about what was important (just like in the immediate aftermath of 9/11).

Why didn't the department provide the necessary leadership? I wish I knew. Were Rahm Emanuel and Geithner against aggressive investigation and prosecution? Geithner has said publicly: "The stuff that seemed appealing in terms of . . . Old Testament justice . . . penalize the venal, would have been dramatically damaging to the basic strategy of putting out the panic, getting growth back, making people feel more confident in the future. . . ." Seemed appealing? Absolutely necessary, in my view. Geithner's statement would seem to indicate that he believes utilitarian outcomes justify overlooking potentially criminal behavior by banks.

I suspect that Attorney General Holder, who always has an ear cocked to the White House, got the essence of Geithner's message. Rahm was well known for making hundreds of phone calls a day, directly or through proxies, to micro-manage the administration. Moreover, friends of mine who worked in the White House confirmed to me that no one in the Justice Department ever made high-level financial fraud cases a priority.

If the White House, Geithner, and Holder thought they faced a binary option—pursue financial fraudsters vigorously (thereby jeopardizing the economic recovery) or feign vigor but actually do nothing besides levying a few paltry fines (thereby not jeopardizing the economic recovery)—they were wrong. Individual executives, not the firms for which they worked, could've been singled out and prosecuted without disrupting the banks' ability to recover. The fact that no individuals were being held accountable left us with a Wall Street thoroughly mistrusted by Main Street.

Of course, government lawyers can point out that they were the only people in a position to see the evidence and to have a preview, from opposing counsel, of the target's defense. Because disclosures were made (they were just buried deep in the prospectuses) and because accountants and lawyers had signed off on the transactions, the Justice Department can assert that prosecution, no matter how aggressive, would've failed. In my opinion, the department was too deferential to the white-shoe law firms defending potential targets: If the highly paid defense team said the target's behavior wasn't illegal, they bought it (or at least believed that a jury would). If Obama had appointed aggressive trial lawyers (and Biden knew plenty of them) to these Justice Department positions and backed their efforts, there's a good chance they would've hunted the worst Wall Street fraudsters relentlessly.

Before Ted left office, he wanted another opportunity to have Breuer, Perkins, and Khuzami testify publicly. In late September 2010, he called them before a second FERA oversight hearing, determined to get answers. Gaveling the hearing to begin, he said: "I will say right now that I'm frustrated." He wanted to know whether the Justice Department had the "infrastructure, personnel and strategies in place" to find criminal conduct on Wall Street. After expressing obligatory praise for how "incredibly hard" government investigators had been working, he asked why there had been no "senior officer or boardroom-level prosecutions of the people on Wall Street who brought this country to the brink of financial ruin?" Looking straight at Breuer, he continued:

> Why is that? Is it because none of the behavior in question was criminal? Is it because too

much time passed before investigators got serious, so the trail has gone cold? Is it because the
law favors the wealthy and powerful? Or is the
explanation more complex? Are there systemic
challenges that the agencies are finding difficult
to overcome? . . . Is the fine print exculpatory?

Predictably, Breuer dodged Ted's questions and instead proffered generalities ("The department has engaged in a robust and comprehensive investigation"),
statistics on garden-variety financial fraud cases ("between October 2009 and June 2010, nearly three thousand defendants were sentenced to prison for financial
fraud, and more than sixteen hundred of these defendants have received sentences of greater than twelve
months"), and details of recent cases that had nothing to
do with Wall Street and the financial crisis ("on September 15, 2010, Nevin Shapiro, the former CEO of Capital
Investments USA Inc., pleaded guilty in Newark, New
Jersey, to fraudulently soliciting funds for a non-existent
grocery distribution business"). Sitting behind Ted, I
tried hard not to roll my eyes as Breuer touted the successful prosecution of a grocer for a small-time New Jersey Ponzi scheme. He was ducking the main issue and
continuing to assure Ted and the rest of the committee
that the department was being "thorough" and "robust"
in its effort to bust big-time fraudsters.

To the department's credit, the U.S. attorney in the
Eastern District of Virginia, Neil MacBride (a former
Biden chief counsel), had recently indicted Lee Bentley

Farkas, the former CEO of Taylor, Bean & Whitaker Mortgage Corporation (TBW). TBW was once one of the largest private mortgage companies in the United States. Farkas was charged with perpetrating a massive fraud scheme that resulted in losses exceeding $1.9 billion and that contributed to the failure not just of TBW, but also of Colonial Bank, one of the fifty largest U.S. banks before its collapse in 2009 (in June 2011, Farkas was sentenced to thirty years in prison and fined $38.5 million). That was the only significant case Breuer could point to.

In his testimony, Khuzami was more clear and detailed. He at least separated the cases the SEC had brought into two categories: those related to the financial crisis (like civil actions against Goldman Sachs, Citigroup, State Street, and several other major players) and those unrelated to the crisis (like Ponzi schemes and insider trading). Khuzami stressed that in the last nine months the SEC had brought enforcement actions (and obtained hundreds of millions of dollars in settlement penalties) against companies and individuals that:

- concealed from investors the risks and exposures from subprime mortgage-based securities;
- concealed business strategies that heightened the risks relating to mortgage-based securities;
- failed to disclose to investors the involvement of adverse parties in structuring complex mortgage-based securities;

- concealed that investment funds contained high-risk mortgage-based securities;
- marketed high-risk mortgage-based securities while secretly divesting themselves of their own holdings.

There they were. All the illegal behaviors that we had long believed had taken place during the financial crisis. But the SEC was dealing with these cases by bringing civil actions, which only have to be proved by a preponderance of the evidence (unlike criminal cases, which only the Justice Department can bring and every element of which must be proved beyond a reasonable doubt). Moreover, the SEC was settling these cases (and levying comparatively trifling fines) rather than proving the allegations in court. That meant that the banks didn't have to admit to any wrongdoing, which enhanced their ability to defend themselves against private civil actions and denied the public a sense of closure.

During Q&A, Breuer finally got close to saying something interesting. He explained that "from the simplest to the most complex" case, there must be a "materially false statement" where the defendant "can't point to something" to show his innocence. "Falsehood and criminality" are what we need to prosecute. So why not take us through the obvious potential defendants, I thought, and just come out and say it? This theory wouldn't work against target X because he could point to Y disclosure buried deep in the documents. That theory wouldn't work against target W because W could point to an exculpatory e-mail Z. This would've helped an outraged citizenry to better understand why the Justice Department was repeatedly deciding not to prosecute.

Because we knew that Breuer would say it would be improper to discuss the results of a specific federal investigation, Ted tried to gain clarity by using a hypothetical. He talked about a bank in the mortgage-origination business that, in an effort to maximize market share and raise profits, had decided to secretly relax its underwriting standards to a greater and greater degree, with the result that a large majority of its loans (particularly its riskiest loans to the least qualified borrowers) were liars' loans. He pressed the panel of witnesses, particularly Breuer, for an answer: "What if this hypothetical bank knowingly issues widespread exceptions to its published underwriting standards, while at the same time claiming to would-be purchasers of mortgage securities that the underwriting standards had been substantially complied with?" He waited for an answer, but Breuer deferred to Khuzami as the expert. So Kaufman tried a new tack with Breuer:

> Or suppose [the hypothetical bank] determines that a class of mortgages that it has held for its own investment are likely to default in the near future and seeks to offload these mortgages onto third parties. That might not be a crime, but what if the bank has claimed to purchasers that it has

not selected mortgages for sale based on a belief
that they are likely to default?

Breuer again deferred to Khuzami. Using variations
on his hypothetical, Ted tried repeatedly to achieve a
clearer understanding of the difference between merely
reckless conduct and criminal conduct. But no matter
how Ted framed the question, Khuzami (not Breuer)
simply reiterated the basic elements of an action for a
materially misleading statement or mentioned theories
regarding accounting violations (although with regard
to Countrywide, he did say that the theory was that
the company's executives knew their business model
was deteriorating and allegedly should've disclosed this
as a trend and an uncertainty).

In his effort to help the country understand why
there had only been settlements of civil cases but, despite the available evidence, no criminal prosecutions,
Ted was getting nowhere. And he was getting no assistance from Breuer, who confined himself to generalities.
The Justice Department seemed to have handed the job
of financial-crisis-related fraud to the SEC. For its part,
the SEC seemed to be focusing on resolving allegations
through civil-law settlements and comparatively pain-
less monetary fines. But this approach, I believe, was
the mere semblance of accountability under law. Moreover, it did little to help the country put the financial
crisis behind it or allay its mistrust of Wall Street.

Ted was now more frustrated than before the hearing. But he remained convinced, by what he'd learned

from many sources (including the PSI hearings held by Senator Levin), that serious criminal behavior had occurred as well. And he was determined that it be brought to light:

> Widespread cheating and fraud, of the sort that drove the speculative housing and derivative securities bubbles, are anathema to public confidence in the markets. In order to assure investors, and the public, that we have learned our lessons from the last disaster, we must have a full account of the criminality that led us there.

Ted's voice became husky with emotion as he concluded his remarks. "This November, I will leave the Senate and the task of oversight will fall to my colleagues. I encourage each of you to keep up the hard work, to keep digging into offerings documents, e-mails, board minutes. To keep developing leads through whistleblowers, plea deals and tip hotlines. I am confident that you will."

Despite my concerns, I wanted to believe Breuer's assertion that the Justice Department's investigation was "comprehensive" and "robust." After the hearing, I walked up to him at the witness table and said, "It's always reassuring to hear you say these things publicly." If he was going to come before a Senate committee and sound like Eliot Ness, he'd better produce some significant cases; otherwise, in hindsight he'd look like he'd just been Kevin Costner reading his lines.

Yes, it's difficult to prove criminal intent in cases of financial fraud, especially when a defendant relied on professional advice from accountants and lawyers (and in some cases may even have been acting with the knowledge of the bank's regulator, who was apparently more concerned about the bank's financial soundness than about full disclosure to investors). But we shouldn't outsource the interpretation of fraud laws to a potential defendant's accountant and lawyers. And why haven't prosecutors used provisions in the Sarbanes-Oxley Act, which put in place tough criminal sanctions in the wake of Enron and other cases of massive corporate frauds? In the absence of an aggressive, targeted effort by the Justice Department, we'll never know whether crimes may have been proved beyond a reasonable doubt.

Ted and I had come to the Senate with the idea that the Justice Department should form a number of financial-fraud strike forces. We worked on giving them additional funds, and took Holder and Breuer at their word when they said they would make these cases a top priority. In hindsight, I wish we'd required the department to provide us with a monthly update of how many prosecutors and investigators it had working full-time on different potential cases. Maybe that would've been oversight overkill (and we were also aware of the inappropriateness of a senator asking about particular cases). But the fact is, not enough effort was put into investigation and prosecution.

I also wish Chairman Leahy had taken the lead in

holding the Justice Department's feet to the fire and that other senators had cared more, too. Ted was a freshman senator, transitory, and not on the Appropriations Committee, as Leahy was. We thought we were doing effective oversight, but, when it was over, I felt misled and gamed by the Justice Department.

As I became more and more concerned about the lack of Wall Street prosecution, I asked Ted on several occasions why he didn't just "ask Biden to call Holder and get the debrief on what is going on? If Biden tells you he's convinced that all that should be done is being done, that's good enough for me." Ted, who had forty years of experience in shielding Joe Biden from criticism, just changed the subject. I wasn't close enough to Biden to do it myself. Other Biden insiders would probably explain that the Justice Department is outside Biden's "zone of influence" (the Obama team never gave Biden the opportunity to place his people in the Justice Department or White House Counsel's office). They'd go on to say that, from the beginning of his vice presidency, Biden is lucky not to have been muzzled and rendered irrelevant, and that it's a huge success story that he's been able to do as much as he has. I think that's true, but still a poor excuse. Biden could pick up the phone at any time, call Holder, and ask about resources and the progress on pursuing financial fraud. Biden is a former trial lawyer, former chairman of the Senate Judiciary Committee, and proud of his thirty-six-year history on civil and criminal justice issues. At the height of my frustration at the absence of indictments, I said to Ted: "Why don't you call your friend Joe Biden and tell him to stick a hot poker up the Justice Department? The buck stops one door down from him."

Even as I uttered the words, I knew they were useless. I knew what we were up against. I'd been in these trenches before. I'd watched the relationship between Washington and Wall Street evolve over more than twenty years, and I didn't like it. In the Clinton administration, as special assistant to White House Counsel Abner Mikva, I'd watched Wall Street flex its hypertrophic muscles. And I'd seen how Wall Street can defeat even the president of the United States.

7:

WALL STREET VETOES
THE PRESIDENT

AFTER GRADUATING from law school in 1994, at the beginning of the Clinton era, I wanted to clerk for a federal judge. Despite my disenchantment with Biden, I knew that my relationship with him and his staff was among the best I had to trade on if I was to accomplish that goal, so I started making calls. Mark Gitenstein, formerly Biden's chief counsel and at that time a partner at a DC law firm, knew Abner Mikva, the chief judge of the U.S. Court of Appeals for the DC Circuit, fairly well (they went to the same temple), and he recommended me to Mikva. I flew to Washington for an interview.

As Mikva was showing me his office he pointed to a picture on the wall and asked, "Do you know who she is?" "Eleanor Roosevelt," I replied. Mikva used the question as a proxy for general knowledge and never hired a clerk who couldn't answer it correctly. Mrs. Roosevelt had come to Chicago to campaign for Mikva when he was running for the Illinois legislature. Mikva later represented Hyde Park in Chicago in the U.S.

Congress for several terms before being gerrymandered out of office by the Republican-controlled Illinois legislature. Mikva moved to Evanston and ran again for Congress in 1976. He won by fewer than three hundred votes. The next year, Mikva got the opportunity to meet President Carter and was feeling like something of a VIP until Rosalyn Carter said, "Jimmy, you remember Ab. He barely won."

I'd only been in Mikva's chambers for a few weeks when rumors began to circulate that Clinton might appoint Mikva to be counsel to the president. After the resignation of Bernie Nussbaum, Clinton's first counsel, Lloyd Cutler had joined the White House as special counsel. Now Cutler was leaving, and Clinton's new chief of staff, Leon Panetta, recommended Mikva as a replacement. When the news became official, I couldn't believe my luck. My long-held dream of working in the White House looked like it was going to come true. The only difference was that it would be for President Clinton instead of President Biden. Mikva's other two clerks had already lined up Supreme Court clerkships for the following term and weren't interested. I, of course, wanted desperately to follow Mikva to the White House, but he said he wasn't clear yet about what staff members he could take.

I immediately called Ted: "I need Biden to call Mikva and tell him I'm great and that he should definitely take me with him." Biden was chairman of the Senate Judiciary Committee, and I knew the counsel to the president would want to have a relationship with him. Ted said he'd make it happen right away.

Meanwhile, I did everything I could to be helpful to Mikva. At the time, Clinton was thinking of moving military forces into Haiti. Walter Dellinger, the acting assistant attorney general for the Office of Legal Counsel, faxed Mikva a draft memo arguing that the move did not require congressional approval. Dellinger wanted Mikva's view right away. Knowing that Mikva had published a law review article on the War Powers Act, I asked him whether it would be useful for me to summarize his article, reconcile it with Dellinger's arguments, and add my thoughts. He agreed and found my memo helpful for his response to Dellinger.

I kept on. Unbidden, I drafted a plan to help Mikva manage his transition; it contained a summary of the issues that faced the Counsel's office, the outlines of a communications strategy, and suggestions for organizing his legal team. I was determined to show him that I could add value as a member of his team.

At around this time, Ted called back: "Biden doesn't want to call him." "What?" I asked. "Biden doesn't want to call Mikva. It has nothing to do with you. He doesn't like Mikva. " Livid, I said: "Who cares whether he likes Mikva. This is about me." I was incredulous. I'd kept my word to Biden and waited six years for him to run for president, shed my life as an investment banker in Atlanta like a snake's skin to move to Washington, worked tirelessly on Biden's presidential campaign, stayed loyal to him at his lowest hour, worked tirelessly again for years on his Senate staff and recently had

written a law review article for him. It was time for
Biden to return some loyalty to me. Ted tried to console
me: "Jeff, don't take this personally. Biden disappoints
everyone. He's an equal-opportunity disappointer."

I looked for consolation from a friend who is another former Biden staffer, someone who had worked
for Biden for six years. He said, "Jeff, the difference between Ted Kennedy, who has spent decades promoting
his former staff into government jobs, and Joe Biden,
is Kennedy believes in force projection. Kennedy Democrats share an ideology. Biden is only about himself
becoming president, he doesn't care about force projection, so he never helps his former staff get jobs." In
other words, the late Ted Kennedy cultivated and
promoted staff not just because he was a decent boss,
but because he had an ideological agenda and the staff
served it across Washington. In contrast, Biden is a
pragmatist. His ambitions, I was coming to understand, were mainly about himself.

Yes, I was disappointed, but ultimately it didn't
matter. Mikva offered me a position as his special assistant at my current clerk's salary. Others in the Counsel's office had fancier titles and made far more money.
I didn't care: I was in. And without Biden's help. And
that is how I came to witness Bill Clinton facing down
Wall Street.

It was past nine o'clock in the evening when President Clinton strode into the room. He was dressed im-
maculately in a suit and tie, yet he strongly resembled

an older version of the Arkansas kid he'd once been, perhaps because of the way his face lit up when he saw Bruce Lindsey, his long-time friend and deputy White House counsel. It was as though Mikva and I weren't even there.

The president asked Bruce whether he remembered an old visitor from northwest Arkansas. "Well he was here last night, and I offered to let him stay in the Lincoln Bedroom, and you know what he said to me?" Clinton affected an even deeper Arkansas accent: "Mr. President, I know you think Lincoln was a great president, but if he was so great, why'd we even have to fight that war?" We all laughed, and Clinton continued, "Can you believe that? Half the country wants to see the Lincoln Bedroom, and he didn't want to stay in it."

Clinton turned off the mirth like a faucet. He asked Bruce: "So what have we got?" What we had, as Bruce explained, was the Private Securities Litigation Reform Act of 1995, now before the Senate. A corporate coalition—Wall Street banks and brokers, accountants, insurers, Silicon Valley—wanted the bill, which would make it more difficult to prove securities fraud, passed intact. The bill's opponents felt it would shield securities fraud by these companies. Particularly troublesome to them were provisions regarding the statements companies make about future performance.

The bill's opponents felt that its language threatened their ability to sue for securities fraud when a company's executives talked up the price of its stock by

issuing misleading forecasts while simultaneously selling their own shares. Those behind the bill, however,
wanted to make it harder to prove wrongdoing in such
cases. According to them, whenever a stock's price
dropped, securities class-action lawyers quickly filed
suits against companies in the hope that they would
settle out of court rather than risk losing at trial. Wall
Street and others viewed these suits as extortion. They
wanted increased protection in such cases, but the bill's
opponents felt that the proposed legislation gave Wall
Street and the others too much leeway. Mikva, Bruce,
and I believed some adjustment may have been needed,
but the proposed bill set an almost impossibly high bar,
giving Wall Street and the others too much protection.
The White House was under tremendous pressure.

Just the day before, White House Deputy Chief of
Staff Erskine Bowles, after getting an earful from a
number of CEOs, had taken the West Wing stairs two
at a time on his way to Mikva's office. From my desk
outside the office, I heard Bowles practically yell, "What
the hell are y'all doing to make Silicon Valley so upset
about this bill?" Wall Street, seeking to hide the blue
stock-trader jackets of high finance behind the white
lab coats of high tech, had wisely pushed Silicon Valley
in the vanguard of lobbying the White House. What
we're doing is standing up for a fair outcome, I thought
to myself, as Mikva closed the door behind Bowles.

Afterwards, I begged Mikva to ask to see the president again. I was determined that the White House not
undercut Arthur Levitt, the chairman of the Securities

and Exchange Commission, who was standing up to the bill's authors to force modifications. Levitt was trying his best to gain revisions to the bill so it wouldn't eviscerate private securities-fraud actions, an important supplement to the SEC's own enforcement efforts.

Mikva asked for time on Clinton's schedule, and I quickly banged out a briefing memo for him. When Clinton's scheduler finally called, much later that night, Mikva turned to me and said, "Come on." This would be the only time I would personally brief the president on an issue.

The meeting, which Bruce Lindsey also attended, was in Clinton's personal study in the White House mansion rather than in the Oval Office. That was a plus. Few staffers got to see the study, with its famous painting of Lincoln and his Union Generals with a rainbow in the background. The minus was at that late hour no official photographer would be on duty. So there would never be a picture of me seated on the couch, Leaning Forward to Educate the President on a Momentous Issue.

Bruce provided an overview of the standard in the Senate bill, and I filled in the specifics. The standard required a showing of three elements, connected by an "and." This meant a plaintiff would have to prove all three of the elements to get past a defense motion to dismiss the suit. The president looked at Bruce and me and said "Did y'all say 'and'? They have to show the first two and the third?"

"Yes, Mr. President."

"Well that's just too high." I recognized the "high" as pronounced by a fellow Southerner, with mouth wide open to give the I its full effect. "I've stood out there in Silicon Valley, and I've heard them go on and on about how bad some of these class action suits are, but I can't be in a position where it looks like I'm protecting securities fraud." Clinton even started to mimic the voice of an imaginary radio ad against him on the issue. I was urging him to take this position, so I didn't point out that it was highly unlikely any Republican opponent would try to use it against him.

"I can call Chris if you need me to," the president said, referring to Senator Chris Dodd of Connecticut, the Senate bill's author and then-current chairman of the Democratic National Committee. Dodd was Corporate America's point man in the Senate effort to curb class action securities action suits. Bruce said he'd call him and would keep the president informed.

As the meeting broke up, Clinton told Mikva and Bruce to go next door and say hello to Hillary, the First Lady, who was having dinner with Ann Landers, an old friend of Mikva's from Chicago. We left the president in his study.

While Mikva and Bruce went into the dining area, I stayed in the hallway, amazed that I was standing alone in the White House living quarters. A couple of minutes later, President Clinton exited the study and smiled as he approached me. "Go on in there. Don't be shy," he said, again prolonging the vowel in "shy" a whole note.

"Thank you, Mr. President. I don't really need to meet Ann Landers," I said.

Then, in a moment I'll never forget, the president of the United States looked me in the eye and said, "You think I'm doing the right thing, don't you?" My passion apparently had shown during the briefing. Like most who had trod those historic halls, I turned out to be a yes-man: "Absolutely, Mr. President. You can't undercut the Chairman of the Securities and Exchange Commission on a question of securities fraud."

President Clinton reflected, "Yeah, that's right. And Levitt is an Establishment figure, right?" Clinton was trying to reassure himself that the heat he'd take from Corporate America was worth it because even Levitt, one of its own, thought the legislation went too far. If the president has to think very hard before taking on this kind of fight, I thought to myself, imagine how disproportionately unlikely it is for Washington's lower castes to dare do the same.

"Yes, Mr. President. That's right."

That night, I couldn't sleep. It was intoxicating to have talked to the president. I knew I'd be meeting the next day with a dozen staffers from various White House offices—National Economic Council, Domestic Policy, Legislative Affairs, the Vice President's office, and even the first lady's staff—who had been weighing in on this issue. I'd been arguing with all of them. Most of them had wanted to appease Silicon Valley because its support had burnished the images of Clinton and Gore as forward-thinking, pro-business Democrats.

When the meeting began the next morning, I said: "We met with the president last night," and I laid out his decision. For the first and only time in my life, I felt presidential power surge through my body. It was electric. Every staffer who just the day before had been an obstacle now lay down like a forest blown flat by a nuclear blast. There was no further discussion. Mikva, Bruce, and I had the president's decision. It was time to implement.

I called a staffer in Senator Paul Sarbanes's office. I briefed him that if Sarbanes would offer an amendment that would preserve the viability of a securities-fraud action against company executives who had "actual knowledge" that, a forward-looking statement was fraudulent, the White House would support it. Sarbanes's staffer didn't believe me. Just watch, I said. I'll get you a letter within an hour. Move forward with the amendment.

Sarbanes offered his amendment. As he spoke in the well of the Senate, he held aloft a letter from Mikva stating the White House strongly supported this amendment, which, to be honest, was hardly a radical notion. All it said was that company executives who knowingly lie about future performance won't be protected from securities-fraud lawsuits.

The vote began, and it looked for a while like we were going to win. Then Dodd started working his fellow senators. It soon became apparent it was going to be a tie. Finally, Dodd voted against the amendment, which failed by one vote.

Bruce had called Dodd and told him that President

Clinton had personally requested this change. Yet Dodd still opposed the amendment. He sided with Republicans against a vast majority of Democratic senators. Dodd, for years one of the biggest recipient's of financial services industry campaign contributions, was too deeply in the pocket of Wall Street and the accountants to go against them. Admittedly, many of the Democratic senators who supported the amendment had long received campaign contributions from securities class-action lawyers.

Dodd's excuse was that the issue could be worked out when the slightly different versions of the bill passed by the House and the Senate were reconciled in conference before being sent to the president. Bruce was deeply disappointed that Dodd had voted against the president. I was outraged. It was my first experience of how Wall Street, accountants, and insurance companies could combine to bend Washington to its will. I knew the accounting industry—because it had activated its professional members in virtually every state—had been a particularly effective fundraising machine. Partners at the big accounting firms had spoken about the bill with hundreds of members of Congress and dozens of senators at campaign donor events across the country. Accountants were often the deep pockets targeted by class-action lawyers after the fraudulent company those same accountants had audited each year had turned feet upwards.

My role at this stage became to negotiate a compromise provision while reporting to Bruce. I never met with a senator or representative or their staff; all of my negotiations were directly with the corporate coalition. Because I wasn't an experienced attorney (I'd graduated from law school only a year earlier), I relied on input from two respected academics: John Coffee of Columbia Law School and Donald Langevoort, then at Vanderbilt Law School. I called them frequently for objective advice on how judges would apply the various drafts of the provision.

During the negotiations, I was invited to hold a video conference call with the general counsels of Apple, Hewlett Packard, and five other Silicon Valley firms. At one point, one of the general counsels said, "Jeff, where is all this fraud you're so worried about?" I'm not claiming to have been clairvoyant. But Enron, WorldCom, Arthur Andersen, and other prominent cases of systematic fraud would soon prove that questioner's confidence in corporate rectitude to be ill-founded.

After weeks of discussion, I offered a compromise. The White House would agree to a two-pronged approach. The standard would be "actual knowledge" that a forward-looking statement was false, or a higher "willfulness" standard if the statement had been accompanied by "bespeaks caution" language: in other words, if the statement was followed by a description of risk factors and a warning to investors not to rely on the prediction's accuracy.

The coalition never accepted or rejected my proposal, and the impasse dragged on for months. Mikva, who just a year before had hired me as one of his judicial clerks, even joked at one of the Counsel's office staff meetings, "Who knew that Jeff would become a household name on Wall Street?"

By this point, Mikva, Bruce, and I had also established that the White House was opposed to the product liability reform bill—which targeted the standards governing private suits for negligence against manufacturers of faulty products—making its way through Congress. Mikva was fielding phone calls from a handful of Democratic senators, including Jay Rockefeller, who were furious that White House lawyers were placing roadblocks in front of that bill, too.

Meanwhile, Arthur Levitt at the SEC had been under siege to soften his position on the securities-fraud bill. During a visit to meet with Mikva, Levitt told me how personally offended he was by the insulting language and the threat of SEC budget cuts that Dodd and other senators had used when they berated him by telephone. These were important issues; the SEC should've played a leading role in crafting the standards in the bill. Instead, Congress was bullying the SEC chairman to support legislation slanted toward the interests of a corporate coalition that had raised millions of dollars for members of the House and Senate.

The bill emerged from conference. Now the question became: Would Clinton sign it? Mikva, Bruce, and I lobbied hard for a veto. We encouraged independent legal scholars—who didn't have a dog in the fight—to write letters to Clinton. As it turned out,

Clinton was very close to John Sexton, the president of New York University and a securities law expert. Sexton spoke to the President and urged him to veto, which Clinton did. Some have speculated that Clinton wanted to have it both ways: he vetoed the bill, but also signaled to Dodd that he wouldn't be overly displeased if two-thirds of Congress voted to override it. I don't know whether that's true or false.

Regardless, that's exactly what happened. Even Ted Kennedy, the great champion of civil rights and liberties, who had assured plaintiffs' groups that he was with them, flipped and went along with the corporate coalition and voted to override Clinton's veto. For Bruce, Mikva, and me, the defeat was devastating. The next morning, Dodd was quoted on the front page of the *Washington Post* as saying that Clinton's veto had been the result of "poor staff work." For unrelated reasons, Mikva left the White House a short time later. Because he'd brought me with him, I followed him out the door.

In his second term, President Clinton made mistakes—deregulating the financial services industry, supporting the repeal of the Glass-Steagall Act, and leaving derivatives transactions unregulated—that would, within a decade, have devastating consequences. Once upon a time, though, in 1995, we had a president who—with the support of his advisors—was willing to do the right thing and stand up to Wall Street, which even then had already taken over most of Washington.

8:

INSIDE THE INFLUENCE INDUSTRY

IN EARLY 1997, it was time for Jack Quinn, Mikva's replacement as counsel to the president, to leave the White House. He turned to his colleague Sheri Sweitzer, asking who should join him to start a law practice at his old firm, Arnold & Porter. "I need someone who really knows how to make his boss look good," Sheri said, "How about Jeff?"

After leaving the White House, I'd joined Covington & Burling, a top DC law firm, ostensibly to practice appellate litigation but actually, or so it seemed to me, to rack up as many billable hours as possible for the firm. I was miserable. Jack's call was a godsend. It started a new and very different chapter of my Washington life.

In my new career as a lobbyist, I dropped Biden's name shamelessly. Perpetuating the myth that I was close to him enhanced my cachet and standing in Washington. It was like a political version of codependency. Biden's slights could be painful, but it seemed too late to break ranks, even though the relationship never actually helped me when I went to work with Jack. Biden never lifted a finger for me or for one of my clients. Every evening after work, he rode a train back to his home in Wilmington. He's a family man and indeed an ordinary Joe. Unlike most of Congress, he hardly ever schmoozed with the Permanent Class. He did the best he could to stay as far away from it as possible.

Not me. When I started lobbying, I was thirty-eight years old and had few assets: no house, a cheap car, and a four-figure bank account. I'd made modest salaries in government and spent all my Wall Street savings on law school. I'd stayed in Washington for reasons that had little to do with issues or ideology; for me, it was now mainly about establishing a DC profile, making money, and helping Democrats beat Republicans.

My timing was great—that is, if I wanted to make a lot of money in DC's private sector. The money spent by corporations to influence Washington at least tripled in my twelve years as a lobbyist. In 1997, when I started, politically active organizations reported $1.26 billion in direct lobbying expenses. When I left to rejoin government in 2009, that figure had increased to $3.47 billion. Controlling for inflation, that's almost seven times the estimated $200 million in lobbying expenses reported in 1983. Approximately fourteen thousand organizations are now listed in the directory of Washington representatives, double the roughly seven thousand listed organizations in 1981.

These figures don't capture how much Corporate

America spends on public affairs and public relations, which don't require public reporting. Hybrid firms often take a fee from clients and decide that half was for lobbying and that half was for public relations like communications and media strategy (which isn't subject to reporting requirements). And there are other ways a corporation or trade association can spend money in Washington to affect government outcomes, such as hiring law, analytical, grassroots, and third-party-outreach firms (which also isn't subject to disclosure). In other words, the total amount of money being showered on former (and future) public servants is vast and unknowable.

Washington makes decisions that have an economic impact worth millions of dollars to individual companies, billions to sectors of the economy, and trillions to the economy as a whole. That's why it makes sense for big business to flood Washington with cash (and do the same thing on a smaller scale in state capitals across the country).

The problem isn't new. In 1913, Woodrow Wilson wrote: "If the government is to tell big business men how to run their business, then don't you see that big business men have to get closer to the government even than they are now? Don't you see they must capture the government, in order not to be restrained too much by it? Must capture the government? They have already captured it."

When the corporate pie tripled in just over a decade, so much money was being spent in Washington that it completely changed the culture. Just like on Wall Street, when the benefits available to professionals sky-rocketed, and the costs of certain behaviors or norms diminished, people rationally started making different choices. The ranks of lobbyists swelled (as did the po-tential wealth available to former public servants), and the sophistication of corporate campaigns intensified.

At Arnold & Porter, Jack charged clients a flat retainer with a minimum one-year contract. The monthly fee, which ranged from $20,000 to $40,000 (but sometimes higher), depended on the complexity and intensity of the assignment. Jack was an entrepre-neurial lawyer who had no interest in methodically keeping timesheets and billing on an hourly basis.

Jack saw the enormous value of Washington coun-sel, particularly for companies engaged in transactions that required regulatory approval. Investment bankers charged huge fees, often earning a percentage of the successful deals they advised or underwrote. So why, Jack wondered, shouldn't Washington lawyers, who had as much or more to do with a deal's ultimate suc-cess, be paid just as handsomely? It took chutzpah, which Jack had. Soon, a wave of mergers came along that permitted us to test his theory.

One of them was SBC's first attempt to acquire AT&T. It had been less than a decade since the Justice Department had forced "Ma Bell" to spin off seven re-gional Bell operating companies, one of which was Southwestern Bell Company, which had shortened its name to SBC. Headquartered in San Antonio, Texas,

SBC was a longtime client of Arnold & Porter. When SBC began thinking about acquiring AT&T, it knew the bold, audacious move probably would strike the public and Washington regulators as difficult to swallow. So SBC assembled a team, including Jack, to devise a government- and public-relations strategy.

SBC's general counsel offered Jack a fee of $100,000 for one month's work, knowing that the deal would require an immense effort on our part with key decision makers. Even though my salary was determined by Arnold & Porter's rigid pay structure for associates and not by Jack's success, it was obvious I'd joined a lucrative practice.

Our first Arnold & Porter team meeting revealed the difference between the flat-retainer and hourly billing mindsets. The first instinct of the firm partners who were paid hourly was to make a long list of every possible task that the firm's lawyers would need to perform. Jack and I, in contrast, had only one thought: to meet immediately with Fritz Hollings (chairman of the Senate Commerce Committee) and Reed Hundt (chairman of the Federal Communications Commission). Why? Because either of them could pronounce the deal stillborn on the day of its announcement. Billing on retainer gave us the incentive to devote our efforts to those strategies and contacts that would maximize the likelihood of success, not to maximize the legion of lawyers whose hours we could bill.

Sure enough, word of the possible deal leaked out before SBC could announce it (or unleash us to make contacts). The press reaction was overwhelmingly negative, and Reed Hundt was almost instantly quoted as saying such a merger would be "unthinkable." SBC's growth ambitions suffered a temporary setback. But Jack's model of high-dollar retainer fees had been vindicated. The hourly lawyers barely did any billable work, while Jack pocketed a $100,000 fee.

In the early months of our new practice, Bell Atlantic was trying to acquire Nynex. Like SBC, Bell Atlantic and Nynex were Baby Bells created when the Justice Department broke apart the original AT&T monopoly. Combining Baby Bells would therefore be viewed skeptically by the department. About this time, I happened to have lunch with Aubrey Sarvis, an old friend and fellow Southerner who was then head of government relations for Bell Atlantic. More than an hour of chitchat passed before we began discussing the Bell Atlantic–Nynex deal, in which Aubrey was immersed. Soon, our talk turned to Joel Klein, who had been Mikva's deputy in the White House counsel's office before becoming principal deputy assistant attorney general of the Antitrust Division and then assistant attorney general, the top man for antitrust review in the Clinton administration.

I mentioned that I'd worked closely with Joel in the White House and thought he was very smart and a good guy. My words were guileless. I hadn't yet become a voracious new-business seeker who tried to turn every friend into a client. That would come later. On that day, Aubrey was just a friend, and I was happy to talk.

Aubrey leaned forward and probed me for more information about Joel. I told him all I knew: the work Joel and I had done together, how Joel thinks, how he analyzes issues. To be honest, I didn't have any earth-shattering insights into the mind of Joel Klein. But for Aubrey, whose company had a multi-million-dollar deal before Joel, any intel was worth knowing. He interrupted me only to call Bell Atlantic's general counsel and explain my relationship with Joel. A few minutes later, we were in a cab to go meet with the general counsel at his office in Arlington, Virginia. And the general counsel had soon heard enough to want to hire Jack and me to help with the Nynex deal. I'd brought in my first client. Jack was pleased.

My first assignment was to call Joel, let him know I was working on the Bell Atlantic team, and ask him for a status update. He was amused: "I suppose it's good that several of my friends are going to make some money off this deal, but Bell Atlantic could hire my mother, and it wouldn't make a difference in how we analyze it." I hadn't thought it would make a difference. But at least Joel had taken my call. What's more, he gave me a carefully worded status update that I could take back to my new client. In Washington, that's worth something. Bell Atlantic was paying Arnold & Porter $25,000 a month for a minimum of a year for Jack and me to make such calls. And do meetings. At some point, the Bell Atlantic lawyers had their opportunity to present their case directly to Joel and the other top Antitrust Division lawyers. Bell Atlantic dragged me along to the meeting, even though I didn't have a speaking role.

After the meeting, Joel pulled me aside to say hello. "These guys weren't going to let you say anything?" That was a hard but good lesson. If you go to a meeting as an ornament, but don't argue the substance of your client's position, you lose credibility with the government official you asked for the meeting.

In those early months I worked with Jack, I began to think that his advice and counsel were exceptional. And from where the client was sitting, oftentimes clueless about the inner workings of government, worth the extravagant sums he was being paid. For two-and-a-half years, Jack had been the vice president's chief of staff and, for almost two years after that, the then-current president's counsel. Clinton had seen a late-night rerun of Jack testifying before the Whitewater Committee chaired by Senator Alfonse D'Amato. The next morning when jogging, Clinton reportedly asked an advisor, "Did you see Jack Quinn before the D'Amato Committee?" Clinton thought Jack was tough (what he wanted in his next counsel), and so he hired Jack away from Gore (who was none too pleased).

On Jack's office wall, he kept a picture of Clinton and Gore, with Jack walking between the two of them in the hallway of the Old Executive Office Building. Clinton was leaning his head over to say something funny in Jack's ear, Gore was leaning across Jack to hear what Clinton was saying, and all three were smiling and laughing like middle-aged college chums. It was a

priceless picture, and one that every client and potential client gazed at with awe, as did I. Few if any people
for hire in Washington had Jack's experience at the
highest levels of our government.

In meeting after meeting with clients and potential
clients, Jack held them (and me) in rapt attention.
Time once referred to him as "the savvy Jack Quinn,"
and savvy he was. He had an uncanny ability to listen
to a client's description of a challenge, absorb it, think
about it for a few minutes, and then lay out in clear
and concise prose the parameters of the key issues—
and the beginnings of how to assess it in a tailored,
strategic framework.

Then, inevitably, Jack would turn the problem
around or inside out and look at it from a different perspective. He rarely followed the conventional path. He
liked to reverse assumptions, challenging the CEO to
try thinking about a matter from the exact opposite approach. Oftentimes that led either to key insights or to
a strategic or tactical idea that no one in the room had
thought of previously. I was becoming a huge fan. I
genuinely believed: This is valuable Washington counsel. We can sell this and make a lot of money.

Jack was particularly valuable in a crisis, when the
situation was chaotic and uncertain. For years, the
Clinton White House had careened from one crisis to
the next, and Jack had excelled in that White House.
His credibility on crisis management issues was therefore extremely high. This is, obviously, useful. At times
of stress, the CEO and other top officers of a company

living through a crisis could say to the Board of Directors: "We hired Jack Quinn, and he's the best, and he says we should do X, Y, and Z." It's the analogous reason companies hire the most prestigious law firms: Regardless of what advice one gets, if things turn out badly, the company executive can always say "We hired the best firm in DC."

At Covington & Burling, I had drifted into the realm of issues involving Silicon Valley. I had worked on a brief arguing that the export controls on encryption (which scrambles data and turns it into unintelligible code) raised First Amendment issues, as encryption essentially is commercial speech. Furthermore, as a former math minor in college, I innately grasped the Silicon Valley argument that encryption is mathematics—even if sophisticated math used to write computer code—and that any attempt to stop math from spreading beyond our national borders was futile. The Swiss and Japanese were already selling sophisticated encryption beyond the levels permitted by U.S. export controls, and so the U.S. government (the argument went) was needlessly hamstringing the leadership of U.S. information technology industries and products.

I told Jack I believed this was the leading issue for Silicon Valley, and that we should go to Northern California and target Silicon Valley companies as clients, to help them devise a strategy for addressing the legitimate national security concerns at issue. Our timing was perfect, as the normally fierce Silicon Valley competitors (Microsoft, Oracle, Intel, Sun

Microsystems, and others) were for the first time talking amongst themselves about organizing an encryption-export reform coalition to lobby Washington and shape the media debate. Jack and I did a round of meetings with all of these companies and were close to being hired.

The Business Software Alliance—the trade group in Washington—was taking the lead in forming the coalition and hiring consultants. Eventually, after we made another round of pitches to BSA executives, the coalition hired Jack to be the lead Democratic consultant and a guy named Ed Gillespie to be the lead Republican.

I had never heard of Ed. It was 1999, and I soon learned that he had been a longtime aide to former House Majority Leader Dick Armey. As policy and communications director for the House Republican Conference, Ed was among those who had drafted the Contract with America, the 1994 campaign platform which (at least in hindsight) was given credit for the Republican gain of fifty-four seats and, for the first time in forty years, control of the House of Representatives. Ed had also worked for Haley Barbour at the Republican National Committee, and after leaving Armey's staff, had opened Policy Impact Communications, a public relations firm that was a subsidiary of Barbour's lobbying firm.

Ed is a typical blue-collar Irishman, even given to calling his male friends "laddie." His father had been wounded in World War II and awarded a silver star, and he then went on to run a bar in New Jersey for many years. Ed was no Country Club Republican. His first job on Capitol Hill was as a Senate parking-lot attendant. Ed was easy to like and had an extremely affable manner.

Jack, Ed, and I were Irish and had been raised from modest upbringings. Jack's father had worked for the power company in New York City for forty years, and my father had never made more than $50,000 a year while working as a chemical engineer for the Army Missile Command. Over the next decade, Jack, Ed, and I went on to make many millions of dollars together. I'm convinced the success of our partnership and friendship was rooted in our shared Irish ethic of hard work and common decency toward one another. Plus Jack and Eddie liked to laugh.

It didn't start smoothly, however. At one of the first organizational meetings, with representatives from each of the major Silicon Valley firms, I made a point and Ed tried to silence me. I stood up to him and made my point again, and we had a brief argument in front of all the clients. Because this was a Republican and a Democratic consultant clashing on the first day, it began to look as if a bipartisan approach to working together was going to be rocky. At the next meeting, however, to my great surprise, Ed publicly apologized to me and granted that the central point I was making had been correct. I don't even know if I had been right, but Ed's willingness to be humble and conciliatory in front of the group spoke volumes about him.

The Jack-and-Ed strategy for encryption reform was that, to accomplish a complex objective in Washington, one needs a multifaceted campaign. In the old days, lobbying had been about getting to the right decision-maker. By 1999 (and even more so today), power in Washington had become far more diffuse. The key to success, Jack and Ed explained, was an effective and sustained communications strategy built on a winning message—backed by well-marshaled substantive advocacy—and delivered through multiple channels targeted at multiple audiences.

Lobbying of Congress—done effectively by both Democrats and Republicans, at the committee and leadership level—is just one channel for delivering the message. Working to shape the media's view of the issue is another, critically important component. Decision-makers read and are greatly affected by news reports, columns, and editorials. Moreover, an aggressive grass-roots campaign to pressure targeted members of Congress in their home districts was part of our strategy and is now commonplace. A campaign needs a Web-based presence and online communications strategy. Finally, especially on a matter as complex as encryption export controls, one must devise and coordinate an effective approach to shaping the views of the multiple agencies inside the administration, which each have a stake in the issue.

As one can tell, all this can add up to a complicated and expensive affair. It makes great sense to hire strategic masterminds with great contacts in government and the media and long experience in Washington (like Jack and Ed) to coordinate a years-long, multi-million dollar effort.

Once immersed in the issues, Jack, Ed, and I agreed fairly quickly on what would be the tipping point. We'd never win until a critical mass of the national security "community"—writ large, including outside experts and former government officials—adopted the view that attempts to control encryption were futile. The government's emphasis should be on gaining the industry's help to increase the sophistication inside our national security agencies at countering the uses of strong encryption, so the U.S. government can still spy effectively on America's enemies. We could lobby and "spin" until we were blue in the face, but if the national security community was against us, we'd remain stymied. The high-tech industry needed to be a responsible partner and help the government to develop cutting-edge solutions to address an important national security challenge.

That's what we communicated all over Washington for the next two years. It was an intense effort on many fronts, but it led to a complete success. The Clinton administration issued liberalized rules for export controls, and Silicon Valley was happy with us. I had become a successful lobbyist, the junior partner to one of DC's most respected wise men.

9:

CAPITAL OF HYPOCRISY

IN THE MIDST of the encryption campaign, the Monica Lewinsky scandal broke, leading to the Ken Starr investigation. In retrospect, it's difficult to believe how obsessed the media (and, later, Republicans in Congress) became in 1998 with the possible impeachment of President Clinton. One measure is that Jack, as a former White House Counsel, appeared on a major Sunday news program—*Meet the Press, Face the Nation, This Week*—to defend President Clinton ten Sundays in a row. For one year, Washington debated whether the Lewinsky scandal and the president's statements were a threat to the rule of law.

Jack got so many TV invitations he couldn't begin to handle them all. This was a good thing for our business; as impeachment began to unfold, other Democratic lobbyists started to scramble for TV invitations to defend Clinton. One day, a producer for CNN's *Crossfire*—hosted at that time by Pat Buchanan from the right and Bill Press from the left—called, asking if Jack could appear that night. Jack had a conflict, so he and I talked, and he suggested that I do the show. After all, I too had served in the White House counsel's office and had been following the Starr investigation as closely as Jack, helping him to prepare for his TV appearances. I called the CNN producer, told him Jack had a conflict, and asked: how about me? I told him my background, he asked me a few questions about what I thought, I gave him my views, and he said, "Okay, let me check, and I'll call you back." Thirty minutes later, I was invited to the CNN studio.

I was extremely nervous as I sat in the makeup chair, waiting to be led to the set. Pat Buchanan dropped by, said hello, and was very friendly. I can barely remember the actual show, it went by in a blur. Later, a friend who watched said I was like a matador with a red cape that had "Clinton" written across it, and Buchanan was a bull, chasing me around a bullring. One of my clients, a Republican, told me he and his wife were watching. Surprised to see an unknown defending Clinton and critiquing Starr, and before her husband could tell her who I was, she turned to him and said, "Who's that son of a bitch?"

After the show, the e-mails poured in, not just from friends in DC, but from Alabama and even from random college friends across the country. It really hadn't mattered what I had said, people had seen me on *Crossfire*, defending the president of the United States. As one of my oldest cousins in Mobile, a Republican, said to my parents: "If you go up against Pat Buchanan and acquit yourself well, you're playing with the big boys."

Regardless of how I performed, I was off to the TV

races. All the shows were calling for Jack, and, when he didn't have time or want to do them, I pitched myself. "Have you ever done TV before?" the young assistant producers would ask. "I was just on *Crossfire* last week," I'd say. "You're booked." Next was *Geraldo Live!*, CNN's *Burden of Proof*, and several other now-defunct cable news shows. I was a B-list talking head.

Jack was scheduled to be on *Meet the Press* (or simply "Meet," as it is known by the Washington cognoscenti) the next day. One of the producers called me: "Jack is in New York today because his mother had a heart attack." I had no idea. Jack had not called me. "He suggested that you fill in for him tomorrow on the show." I was immediately seized with panic. CNN and MSNBC cable shows are one thing, but appearing on a major Sunday show was in a completely different league. I only had a minute to decide before she would simply hang up and find someone else, more than eager to appear. I said okay, thinking to myself this might be the only time in my life I ever get a chance to be on *Meet the Press.*

The producer told me she'd send a car to pick me up at home at 7:00 a.m. the next day, as the show tapes at 8:00 a.m. I'd be on with several others, primarily the lawyer for the Secret Service agents Starr had just subpoenaed to get their testimony about what they'd seen and heard while protecting President Clinton, an unprecedented and potentially very disruptive move by a prosecutor. Other participants in a roundtable discussion would be Stuart Taylor, then with *Legal Times;*

Jonathan Turley, a law professor at George Washington University who had been on TV repeatedly urging a hardline approach to the impeachment of Bill Clinton; and former White House Chief of Staff Leon Panetta, who would appear remote from a California studio.

That Saturday night, I had heart-pounding anxiety like I had never felt before. In fact, I was terrified and deeply regretted my decision to do the show. Jack called me from his mother's bedside (she was doing fairly well) and did his best to calm me down. "Just think up and memorize four short speeches making four different points you want to make. Then, whatever Tim Russert asks you, find a way quickly to pivot into one of those brief speeches. And try to make all four during the show and not get shut out by the other guests talking over you." We talked about what the four points might be.

I thought that was great advice, so I stayed up late into the night writing out my little speeches and practicing them over and over again (out loud) until I could deliver them smoothly. I remembered from moot court during law school that even when I thought I knew exactly what I wanted to say, until I'd practiced saying it out loud many times, I'd search and stumble for words. On the other hand, I didn't want to sound too canned and rehearsed. I was determined not to pivot awkwardly if the question didn't fit with one of my prepared answers.

The car arrived the next morning with a little NBC sign in the window. I was disappointed that none of my neighbors were awake and outside to see me get into the car. Once at the studio, I waited with the other guests in the green room. William Safire and Doris Kearns Goodwin were having a little fruit together. After I introduced myself, Safire said, "Have some fruit, *Meet the Press* always has great fruit." For a second I thought about saying, "*Face the Nation* wouldn't sell you a pastry," but there was no faking it with Safire and Goodwin: they knew I was a rookie.

A staffer led me onto the set and sat me next to Tim Russert, who was friendly, and, in the few minutes before we went on air, chatted amiably with me and the other guests. Turley was on my right, Stuart Taylor next to him, and Michael Lieber, the lawyer for several Secret Service agents, sat across the table. The show's theme song began, and it wasn't long before Russert soon turned to me: "You worked for the White House counsel's office. What is the White House take on all this?" I was taken aback that Russert had introduced me as a White House mouthpiece, when I had spoken to no one at the White House in preparation for the show. I blurted out: "I haven't worked for the White House in two years."

Then I went on the attack, accusing Starr of being on a "fishing expedition" and of casting a "wide dragnet" inside the White House, searching for "corroborative circumstantial evidence of whether the president may have made a misleading statement in a deposition in a civil suit that was dismissed by the court more than two years ago." That was a mouthful but came out without a hitch. Later in the show, I got in another whack, reminding people that Starr's initial charge was to discover whether obstruction of justice had occurred in Whitewater or the Lewinsky matter, and "so far on both fronts he has drilled down and come up with only a dry hole." Finally, I accused Starr of overstepping his bounds, doing the "dirty work" for Congress, when under the Independent Counsel statute, as soon as he found evidence that the president *may* have committed a crime, he was supposed to lateral the issue to the House of Representatives. "In this country, it is the democratic process that elects our presidents, and it is the democratic process—through our elected offi-cials—who should decide whether the investigation of a president for misconduct should be pursued." I pre-dicted that the House of Representatives would not im-peach Clinton for lying in a civil deposition about a sexual liaison (this proved to be an accurate forecast, as the impeachment grounds later voted by the Republi-can House were based on Clinton having lied to a grand jury, a foul that had not yet occurred during my appearance on *Meet the Press*). Russert turned to Panetta and asked him if he agreed with me. I prayed that Panetta wouldn't say, "That man is an impostor, I worked in the White House, and I don't recognize him from Adam." Thankfully, Panetta didn't say that, but instead concurred.

After the show, I was pleased. I had even fought back when Turley had tried to talk over me, saying that my analogy to lying about golf scores was dangerous because we shouldn't let anyone lie about anything when under oath. Impeachment, I said, was a judgment call by elected officials, and no one sitting around a table at *Meet the Press*—not me, not Turley—can claim to know what is an impeachable offense. Only the House of Representatives can decide that question. I thought I was effective in telling Turley to stop pretending to be the moral arbiter of presidential wrongdoing.

Once I was back at my apartment, the show came on, where I could watch myself as it was broadcast across Washington. Soon phone calls and e-mails started coming in. The reviews were unanimously positive. Jack even called from his mother's bedside and said I'd hit a home run. A couple of reporters I knew told me it was an A performance. If you'd asked me whether I wanted to do it again or was happy with the one in the can, I'd have taken the one in the can.

For the next week, everyone I saw in Washington had seen it and complimented me on it. It was quite an education in the power of the medium, as only a random few had caught me on *Crossfire,* but almost *everyone* had seen me on *Meet the Press.* The invitations from the cable shows went exponential. I was getting my fifteen minutes of fame, as they all wanted me on to explain the White House position. During the next two weeks, I did six or seven shows. My clients started treating me like a rock star. My higher profile was enhancing my value to the private sector. I even got a little cocky and spoke to a *Wall Street Journal* reporter on the record, saying "[the] White House had no vision" when it came to encryption policy. Word got back to me from the White House that, if I hadn't just done such a good job on *Meet the Press,* they would've scalped me for having the brass to criticize the White House in print.

Ed had seen all this and been impressed by the role Jack and I were playing. Even I was making a name for myself. The encryption clients had been impressed as well. Jack's stature and mine were on the rise in the Democratic Party because of impeachment. It was a classic example of how to raise your value in Washington by helping to circle the wagons around Democrats in trouble and shoot to kill at any Republican raiders. Even Republicans respected us for it. As Ed used to say, sometimes in football you look across the line and think, I'd like those guys on my team.

Jack, Ed, and I worked together so well that Ed thought we should combine forces and start our own firm as a group of communications specialists with bipartisan capability to lobby both Congress and the administration. I liked the idea. Arnold & Porter was paying me as a fourth-year associate, and by this point I was thirty-eight years old. I was ready to bolt. Jack, on the other hand, had been at Arnold & Porter for more than twenty years, interrupted only by his White House service. One of the firm's highest paid partners, he was risk averse and said no to the idea. But Ed and I wouldn't give up. We met at a hamburger joint near Arnold & Porter and made a PowerPoint presentation for Jack, which would show him how the new firm would work and how within a year or two he could be making even more money than we guessed he was banking at Arnold & Porter. We made our pitch to Jack with great passion and enthusiasm, and still he said no.

Finally, after months had passed, Jack walked into my office one day and said, "We're leaving the firm." It had finally dawned on Jack that teaming up with a high-profile Republican was the best way to take electoral risk out of our money-making equation. Arnold & Porter had always been a Democratic firm and had some difficulty attracting Republican lawyers. It was the fall of 1999, and 2000 would be the year of a presidential campaign that would put either Al Gore or a Republican in the White House. Ed, a prominent Republican, was urging us to form a partnership. As Democrats, we wanted to be diversified against the risk of a Gore loss.

We made our move, and Quinn Gillespie & Associates (I always joked that I was the ampersand) opened its doors in January 2000. Jack and Ed had decided to split the stake marginally in Jack's favor, and Jack had generously cut me in for a lucrative, though small, percentage. (Later, after George Bush was elected president, Jack immediately offered to equalize shares with Ed.) QGA wasn't the first bipartisan firm in Washington, but we were the first to put communications strategy (messaging and public relations) at the heart of the firm. This was supplemented by a bipartisan lobbying capability that encompassed the administration and both houses of Congress, particularly at the leadership level.

Because the Clinton administration had recently reversed its encryption policy, we started with the momentum of success. All of Jack's and my clients at Arnold & Porter followed us to the new firm, as did Ed's, so we began with a slate of blue-chip clients. We had a strong team that brought together people with superior political acumen, experience, and intel. Jack and Ed were consummate Washington insiders, and their approaches to strategy complemented each other. We had people who had worked at public relations firms. And we had others who were experienced lobbyists with numerous connections on both sides of the Hill (Senate and House) and both sides of the aisles (Democrats and Republicans).

BlackBerrys had just come out, and Jack bought one for everyone at the firm. We stayed in constant contact with one another, immediately sending by e-mail any political intel we had gathered. This gave the whole firm a real-time overview of happenings that might affect our clients. Ed and Jack, who both knew dozens of reporters, would feed them tidbits of intelligence and try to plant or shape stories that would help our clients. At the end of each day, we'd reconvene at QGA and sort through it all, fine-tuning strategies for our client and designing an action plan for the next day.

Jack and I had become very good friends, and I thoroughly enjoyed coming to work with him every day. We were becoming genuinely closer to Ed and our Republican colleagues, as well. Although we were all active for our respective political parties, once we stepped off the elevators at QGA, it was about delivering for our clients so we could all make a lot of money. We joked that we were all members of the Green Party. Ed was a rising star in the Republican firmament. In 2000, he was picked to be the program director for the Republican Convention. Next he spent the fall working directly with Karl Rove and Karen Hughes on the Bush-Cheney presidential campaign. Jack, who'd been asked to work full-time on the Gore campaign, stayed at QGA to hold down the fort. We tried to be useful to Gore with discrete projects and, in Jack's case, as a campaign surrogate on TV.

I noticed a subtle change in my political outlook. Although I wanted Gore to win and even travelled to Wausau, Wisconsin, for the final two weeks of the campaign, I could tell the firm would be well positioned for at least the next four years whether Gore or Bush won. Our motto was "We don't lose sleep on election night." Clients started to pour through the doors.

On election night, Jack was in Nashville with the Gore team, Ed in Austin with the Bush team. As the Florida results flip-flopped and Gore called Bush to retract his earlier concession, Jack and Ed were sending e-mails to each other: "How does it look to you?" Ed played a key role for Bush in Florida during the recount. Jack did TV for Gore, but he and I both chose to stay away from Tallahassee and the Gore legal team, which was already awash in attorneys. After the Supreme Court's controversial decision gave the election to Bush, it was clear that Ed was going to be a hot commodity. A Bush administration wasn't my preference for the country, but it was great for our firm. We had buzz. We had cachet. And then, suddenly, we had trouble. In his final days in office, President Clinton pardoned Marc Rich, an indicted oil trader who was one of Jack's clients.

In 1983, then-U.S. attorney for the Southern District of New York (SDNY) Rudy Giuliani charged Rich with tax evasion under the Racketeer Influenced Corruption Organizations Act (RICO), which is normally used against organized crime. Rather than face the charges, Rich, a billionaire, fled to Switzerland and was thus a fugitive from the U.S. justice system. Rich's legal team, led by Republican Scooter Libby, had for years tried to negotiate with the SDNY for Rich's return to face charges. But the SDNY refused to talk until Rich surrendered himself. In 1999, Rich's legal team hired Jack, who only agreed to help after learning that former Republican Attorney General Bill Barr supported the merits of Rich's case. Jack tried to convince then-Deputy Attorney General Eric Holder to play an active role in the negotiations between the SDNY and Rich. Only later did Rich's legal team decide to try for a presidential pardon.

In early January 2001, I ran into Paul Carey, an SEC commissioner (tragically, he died of cancer just five months later). Apropos of nothing, Paul said: "I hate your new client." I asked which one. "Marc Rich," he replied with distaste. Rich actually wasn't a QGA client. Jack was representing Rich in his capacity as an attorney, and no one at QGA had specific knowledge of Jack's actions on Rich's behalf. But Paul's ire made me realize that the pardon application was receiving high-level attention and that things were heating up. One source of controversy was that Rich, an oil trader, had allegedly done business with Iran, which was then (and is now) proscribed by U.S. law. For many, this alone was enough to disqualify Rich for a pardon (even though the charges had been dropped, presumably because Rich was operating out of Switzerland).

On his final day in office, Clinton granted 140 pardons and several commutations. The list included two convicted felons (who had paid Hugh Rodham, Hillary's brother, $200,000 to help them seek clemency), Susan McDougal (of the Whitewater real-estate scandal), and the President's brother, Roger Clinton (who had been convicted in 1985 of a cocaine-related offense and served a one-year prison sentence). Yet it was the pardons of Marc Rich and his partner Pinky Green that elicited the loudest outcry. Media talking heads declared themselves appalled, former President Jimmy Carter called it "disgraceful," and the Republicans smelled an opportunity to tarnish Clinton's legacy.

Even though Scooter Libby (whom Cheney had just named as his chief of staff) and other prominent Republican lawyers had also worked for Rich, it was

Jack who became the focal point of public and media outrage. Because Jack was a good friend and because the media storm was bad for QGA, I threw myself into the crisis-management effort. Jack needed to get a defense of the Rich pardon into the media. So I helped him write an op-ed for the *Washington Post,* which ran on January 26, 2001, within a week of the pardon. In it, we argued that Giuliani's indictment of Rich was overzealous. It marked the first time that RICO—which Congress had intended for use against the mob and which carries long prison sentences—had ever been used to charge an individual with tax fraud. The oil companies themselves, also accused of hiding profits to evade taxes, had only been fined under civil law. Only Rich had been targeted for criminal prosecution (under a statute that the Justice Department later deemed inappropriate for a tax-fraud case). When the Department of Energy reviewed the Marc Rich transactions, it concluded that his companies had properly accounted for them. Professor Martin Ginsburg of Georgetown University Law School, a leading tax-law expert and the husband of Supreme Court Justice Ruth Bader Ginsburg (he died in 2010), had also been retained by Rich and said that Rich's tax treatment of the oil profits was lawful.

The op-ed was a straw in a gale. No one was interested in the possible merits of Rich's case or the pardon. Jack was being vilified on TV. His reputation suffered, and old friends avoided him. The media barrage was relentless. One day we came back to the office to find voicemail messages from a dozen journalists and TV anchors, including Tom Brokaw, Connie Chung, and Morley Safer. And when it came out that Denise Rich, the ex-wife of Marc Rich, had made a $400,000 contribution to the Clinton Presidential Library the previous May, many concluded the pardon had been a quid pro quo.

I became the only person in America willing to go on TV and defend the Marc Rich pardon. I was careful to say that I hadn't been involved and that Jack had represented Rich in his capacity as an attorney, not as a QGA principal. But I believed it was important for people to understand that Jack hadn't circumvented the Justice Department, that the Justice Department itself had subsequently deemed RICO's use in tax cases to be inappropriate, and that the Department of Energy had reviewed Rich's transaction and ruled it lawful. Although others might contend that Rich's fugitive status disbarred him from a presidential pardon, I believed the facts of the case provided a basis for one and that the presidential pardon power was unlimited. (Privately, I thought it had been a mistake for Jack to seek a pardon for a fugitive, and an even bigger mistake—for obvious political reasons—for Clinton to grant it.)

It was useless. The Republicans wanted blood. Congressional investigators compelled QGA to turn over documents, including e-mails I'd written to Jack and others at the firm after the pardon had been announced. In total, Jack spent nineteen hours testifying before the House Government Oversight Committee and the Senate Judiciary Committee. I sat behind him as part of his counsel. Scooter Libby, who'd represented Rich for a decade and earned hundreds of thousands of dollars in legal fees from the case, was also called to testify (the Republican-led House committee scheduled Libby's testimony for late in the evening, after the TV cameras had left). Libby turned on his former client. Asked whether he believed that Rich was a traitor to the United States, Libby replied, "Yes, I do."

I began to notice that people would react differently based on my own posture about Jack. If someone asked me, "How's Jack doing?" and I responded with "There's a principle here, that every client deserves a lawyer, and Jack was just being a lawyer," then I inevitably would have to suffer through a lecture on how egregious Marc Rich's actions were and that Jack should've known better. If, on the other hand, I responded with, "Oh, this is so terrible, Jack is being destroyed by this," then I would get a different response: "Hey, he was just being a lawyer, he'll come through okay."

If the Republications wanted blood, so did the media. Commentators and columnists (this was before the blogger era) were nearly unanimous in their outrage at, and condemnation of, the Rich pardon. Washington, it seemed, wanted a sacrificial lamb (and, ideally, the shepherd himself: Bill Clinton). The relentless inquisition was conducted in another forum as well. For a year after the pardon, SDNY prosecutors repeatedly required Jack, President Clinton, and others to testify before a specially convened grand jury. Some of them were the same prosecutors who'd been involved in the Rich case. But this made them "parties" to the pardon and essentially conflicted in the matter, I believed. If anyone was going to investigate whether Clinton had been bribed to grant the pardon (an assertion that was dubious on its face), it should've been other prosecutors in another district (though if we'd said this publicly, it might simply have goaded the SDNY to continue harassing Jack).

I'll never forget Jack's strength and grace as he endured, and cooperated fully with, these investigations. His experience was often on my mind when, years later, Ted and I were prodding the Justice Department to investigate financial fraud. I frequently pointed out that the Justice Department had been more relentless with Jack (whose role in the Rich pardon had harmed precisely no one) than it had been with Wall Street executives (whose malfeasance had caused a financial and economic crisis that had harmed millions of people). The same goes for those House Republicans who impeached President Clinton, and who (beyond passing FERA) have remained quiet about prosecuting Wall Street fraud.

Part of me—despite my respect for Jack and Ed, their effectiveness, and integrity—was never fully comfortable that I'd become a lobbyist. It's true that on a personal level lobbying was often exciting, interesting, and challenging. I got to advise top decision makers (CEOs, general counsels, and high-ranking government

officials) far earlier in my career than I would have at
Covington & Burling. In the spring of 2000, for example, I negotiated with Federal Trade Commission
staff and eventually the FTC chairman himself to design self-regulatory principles for a coalition of major
online advertisers. A month later, I presented and defended the principles to a panel of seven state attorneys
general, including those of New York and California.
In short, lobbying, from the beginning, could be pretty
heady stuff. But it could also be pretty stressful and distasteful stuff. It was hard to wait for a return phone call
from the government official I was being paid to deliver
access to or obtain intelligence from (the whole lobbying enterprise hinges on being called back). And it was
stressful (and at times distasteful) to raise money for
elected officials. Not surprisingly, fundraising and return phone calls are interrelated. More of the former
elicits more of the latter.

In 1997, when Jack and I first started at Arnold &
Porter, we did little fundraising. Jack's ties to Clinton
and Gore gave him plenty of access without it. As the
years went by, we began to do more. And as you organize more fundraising events, your name creeps up
the publicly available list of large Democratic contributors, and you become a target for fundraising consultants who've noted your success and want you to do
fundraisers for their senators and members.

With Washington awash in money, it's tempting to
conclude that the whole system is rigged. In reality, the
situation is more complex. In lobbying, for example,

raising money is simply part of the job. Senators and members of Congress continuously call the heads (and the lieutenants) of almost every lobbying firm in DC to ask them to do fundraising events. It's difficult to say no. But if you don't learn how to fend off some of the requests, you'll have little time for anything else. If it's an unimportant member of Congress, you simply dodge the call. If it's a senator whose relationship you don't strongly value, you return the call and say, "I'll help with another one of your events and do the best I can." If it's a member or senator whose relationship you do value, it's only a matter of how much you'll commit to fundraise for the event and when it can be scheduled.

Some lobbyists are fanatical about fundraising. They host as many as two or three events each week. Because a limit exists on how much each person or political action committee can contribute in an election cycle, it's sometimes a mystery to me how they find so much money. I suspect some of these bundlers pay their firm employees at levels where the employees are expected to contribute to the firm's events. Linking those two elements would be a federal crime, but there's little doubt that much of a typical lobbyist's income (derived from corporate clients) goes right back into the fundraising coffers of the senators and members they most frequently lobby.

I've always thought a good career strategy for any lobbyist would be to select four or five key senators—on the most important committees, from states where reelection isn't assured—and become deeply involved in their fundraising and political activities. If you can raise money from some group of pockets or simply facilitate the senator's campaign aides in meeting the right people who can help raise money, you're valuable. But you can't be a one-and-done fundraiser. Your commitment and involvement need to be sustained—and perceived as such.

If you can put that amount of effort into five senators, you'll become their Washington friend. And that means you'll always have access. If they begin to trust you, they'll listen intently when you come to them with a request. Your reputation for being part of their trusted circle of political advisors will grow. As a result, more and more special interests will hire you to help them ask for senatorial favors.

If a company hires enough lobbyists with these kinds of personal relationships established across the Senate and House, on both sides of the aisle, then that company will always have access where it counts and to elected officials eager to be helpful. I've sat around tables and been on conference calls where I was only one of ten or twenty or even thirty lobbyists retained by a company. The roll call alone can take five minutes (thankfully, with a last name at the front of the alphabet, I could stop paying attention after the first minute).

The result of all this strategically maximized lobbying and fundraising effort is that those corporate and Wall Street interests (and their lobbyists) that are most affected by congressional and regulatory decisions are best poised at each lever and pressure point to pursue their interests, whether this is to defend a favorable status quo or to tweak legislation and regulatory rules in their favor. Lobbying is only a subset of a much broader problem: the ability of special interests—due to their ability to raise money for elected officials and to retain lobbyists and former regulators to represent them—to have much greater, more frequent, and more influential access in Washington than ordinary Americans have.

And it's not just about lobbying Congress. Much of what we did was called "conditioning the environment" to influence regulatory decisions. Decades ago, after the parties had made a given case in writing and in person, regulators in Washington would apply the law, behind closed doors, on the merits of that case. Today, the law and the merits are often less important than the power and allies a special interest can marshal in favor of its position. In the end, regulators still make a merit-based decision, but only after giant armies have clashed on Washington's darkling plain—encompassing Congress, the administration, and multitudes of constituent and interest groups—applying as much pressure as possible.

I've been a public servant and a lobbyist. From both of these perspectives, I've always believed that lobbyists play an important intermediary role. They provide advice and intelligence to their clients, and facts, analysis, and advocacy to government officials. While a public servant, I believed governance should be open—in the sense of both transparent and available—to interested parties. I found it quite helpful to have people bringing me the best facts and arguments that supported a particular policy position. Ideally, all competing interests (those in favor of the legislation or policy and those against it) are equally adept and vigorous in their advocacy. You, the government official, listen to their briefings, read their materials, and then make your own well-informed judgments.

The problem arises when the advocacy is asymmetrical—that is, when Corporate America or Wall Street lines up on one side of an issue, and no one (or only a grossly outnumbered, outgunned, and out-organized few) lines up on the other. Only a few public-interest advocates are consistently effective. How could it be otherwise? Only the corporate teams—which are extremely well paid, specially trained, and refreshed with substitutions—never waver or become fatigued or despondent during the game. Imagine Appalachian State lining up against the New York Giants and you'll get some idea of how, in Washington, at kick-off the public interest is a four-touchdown underdog.

10:

THE BLOB

A KING HAS HIS RETINUE, a celebrity his entourage, and Pig-Pen his cloud of dirt. Washington has
The Blob. The Blob (it's really called that) refers to the
government entities that regulate the finance industry—
like the Banking Committee, Treasury Department,
and SEC—and the army of Wall Street representatives
and lobbyists that continuously surrounds and perme-
ates them. The Blob moves together. Its members are
in constant contact by e-mail and phone. They dine,
drink, and take vacations together. Not surprisingly,
they frequently intermarry. Indeed, a good way to maximize your family income in DC is to specialize in financial issues and marry someone in The Blob. Ideally,
you and your spouse take turns: One of you works for
a bank, insurance company, or lobbying firm while the
other works for a government entity that regulates, or
enacts legislation for, the financial industry. Every few
years, you reverse roles: "Sally Striver, staffer on the Senate Banking Committee," so might read a typical notice
in *Roll Call*, "today announced her departure to work
for the Financial Services Roundtable"; inevitably, she's

replaced with someone from the financial industry because, so runs the justification, the committee needs
people familiar with the issues. What you and your
spouse do all the time is share information. After all, no
lobbying restrictions yet promulgated can prevent pil-
low talk between Blob spouses. Actually, marrying The
Blob isn't even necessary. A Blob member can simply
take his or her non-Blob spouse to Blob parties—
convivial gatherings of lobbyists and Wall Street emissaries, SEC and Treasury Department officials—to help
gather and disseminate intelligence. It's a weekly, and
sometimes nightly, occurrence in Washington.

Ted and I quickly learned that, when you take on
Wall Street in Washington, you take on The Blob. We
were fighting deeply entrenched interests and a deeply
ingrained institutional culture. Serendipity gave us
some help. Ted, a religious man, faithfully attended the
Wednesday morning Senate prayer breakfasts. It was
here that he developed close friendships with a number
of Republican senators, who responded to the sincerity
of Ted's faith. Senator Johnny Isakson (R-GA) was one
of them. Isakson and Ted shared an interest in financial
issues, and both had recently received complaints from
constituents about the naked short selling of stocks by
hedge funds and about the SEC's rescission of the
uptick rule.

If you think a stock is undervalued, you can buy in
the belief that its price will rise over time. If you think
a stock is overvalued, you can sell it short in the belief
that its price will drop over time. Selling short involves

selling shares you don't own. If the price does drop, you can make a profit when you buy the stock to cover your short sale (if it rises, you make a loss). For example, you might sell Citigroup at $4.20 in the belief that you can later buy the stock at $4 to cover the trade and make a twenty-cent profit. Hedge funds and other traders are constantly engaged in short selling, which accounts for as much as 50 percent of the daily stock trading volume.

Many ordinary investors, including Kaufman and me, have sold stocks short from time to time. But there's an important difference. When I sell stock short, my brokerage firm makes me borrow the shares of stock before I do the short sale. This ensures that I can deliver the shares at the required time for settlement of the trade. Banks and brokerage houses make a lot of money charging people to borrow stock for short sales.

The SEC rule, however, doesn't require that everyone borrow the stock. A short seller only needs to have a "reasonable belief" that he can locate the stock in time to deliver it at settlement, which happens three days later. Selling a stock without intending to locate it in time for settlement is naked short selling. It amounts to selling shares that don't exist, which increases the supply of a stock in a way that can push its price down.

Since the Depression, the SEC had required short sellers to wait for an uptick in price before selling short. Forcing short sellers to wait for the price to tick up before they sell more shares gives a breather to a stock in rapid decline and helps prevent bear raids, which are essentially attacks on a stock (typically by hedge funds) with the aim of driving down its price to ensure that their short selling is profitable. The uptick rule was in force for nearly seventy years. In 2007, the SEC rescinded it. In Mary Schapiro's confirmation hearings before the Senate Banking Committee, she was asked repeatedly whether she would restore the uptick rule. Schapiro, who took office as SEC chairman in January 2009, all but promised she would.

Nothing happened. So on March 3, 2009, Ted wrote to Schapiro, urging her to take action. On March 16, he and Senator Isakson introduced a bipartisan bill that, if passed, would've required the SEC to take action. Still nothing happened. Growing impatient, on June 29, Ted said in an interview: "I would like Mary Schapiro and the folks over there at the SEC to just do their job. I just would like them to do their job." The next day, *Politico*, a prominent DC-based news Web site, ran a piece headlined, "Ted Kaufman to SEC: Do Your Job."

A fewer days later, in the basement of the Russell Senate Building, I saw coming towards me a Senate staffer whose wife worked directly for Schapiro. From a distance of twenty feet he called out, "Hey, Jeff, you're in the doghouse." He meant: with his wife.

"Why?" I asked.

"That *Politico* piece by your boss."

I was taken aback but tried to downplay the matter. "We just want the SEC to get its work done."

"Remember," he said, "We all wear blue jerseys and play for the Blue Team. I just don't think that helps."

With or without his wife's knowledge, he was implying that Ted, a Democrat, shouldn't criticize an SEC chairman appointed by a Democratic president. His blindly tribal mentality in the face of larger issues (like whether our stock markets were fair to the average investor) angered me, but I let it pass.

Ted usually called me on Saturday mornings (even as he traveled around Delaware) to talk about new ideas and coordinate our plan for the coming week. Since we shared just about everything, I told him what the Senate staffer had said. Kaufman exploded: "You call him back right now, and you tell him I said to go fuck himself in his ear." I had no intention of doing that, nor would Ted want me to when he cooled down. But I laughed a few minutes later when I got a call from Ted's press secretary, who was with him: "I'm glad most people still don't know what Ted looks like. Two elderly ladies were standing nearby when he yelled that."

The pushback from the Blue Team was followed by pushback from The Blob. I received an e-mail from a lobbyist (and former Dodd staffer) who represented a large hedge fund well known for short selling. She warned me that it would be bad for my career if Ted and I went after short selling. She added that Ted and I looked like deranged conspiracy theorists for seeking to explore whether short selling had played a role in the downfall of firms like Lehman Brothers. Let me be clear: The Blob isn't the mob. I didn't fear for my kneecaps. But the hedge fund lobbyist was clearly try-ing to get me to back down by making me wonder whether not backing down would harm my career. Sometime later a friend of mine mentioned my name to a top member of The Blob, Mark Patterson, who used to be a lobbyist for Goldman Sachs and is now Treasury Secretary Geithner's chief of staff. According to my friend, Patterson said, "Yes, Jeff has shown a strong interest in issues outside of his jurisdiction." He meant that my boss, Ted, wasn't on the Senate Banking Committee. The Blob doesn't like it when an outsider drops a brick in their punchbowl.

Ted wanted action. He joined forces with other senators who'd been getting an earful from outraged investors. Staff from our office, Isakson's office, and from the offices of Senators Arlen Specter (R-PA), Chuck Grassley (R-IA), Carl Levin (D-MI), and others (a bipartisan group) convened and asked the SEC's Division of Trading and Markets for a meeting. At the meeting, Senate staffers pointed out that the SEC was ignoring the fact that its short-selling manipulation rule was unenforceable. Hedge funds can spread false rumors about a stock and conduct massive short sales without locating the stock, even if they succeed in de-livering the shares three days after the rumors. They could beat down a stock's price repeatedly. The SEC people said little during the discussion. My impression was that they viewed it as another meeting to endure; after feigning to listen, they could simply continue to do things their way.

Next, we asked for a briefing by the SEC's Enforcement Division. We wanted to learn about the status of its investigation into naked short selling of the stock of Bear Stearns and Lehman. At the briefing, SEC lawyers told us we'd have to be patient and that the investigation would take at least another year. They added that they couldn't give us any details of the investigation but warned us that it's almost impossible to prove intent under the current rule (that is, the reasonable-belief standard). Under this rule, anyone accused of naked short selling can simply say: "I reasonably believed I could find the stock in time." In essence, the SEC lawyers confirmed our view that the rule against naked short selling was unenforceable and that they knew it.

Most stock trades in the United States are cleared by a Wall Street backroom firm called the Depository Trust Clearing Corporation (DTCC). I suspected that the DTCC had extensive data on short selling. After a series of enquiries, I finally arranged for the DTCC's general counsel (Larry Thompson) and one of its managing directors (Bill Hodash) to meet with me in Washington. We'd chatted for about fifteen minutes when Larry startled me by saying, "We want to be part of the solution, and we think we have a proposal that will work."

It turns out that months previously the DTCC had gone to the SEC with a proposed solution to naked short selling: The DTCC would create a computer system in which the actual shares of a stock must first be declimated (more simply: flagged or identified) before a broker could sell shares short. A centralized database would prevent the same shares from being used for multiple short sales. The DTCC believed that such a system would effectively stop naked short selling for the shares it cleared, which represented a vast majority of all shares traded in the United States.

Larry told us that the SEC had received the DTCC proposal months ago but hadn't done any follow-up. Instead, the SEC had asked Larry whether he was sure that the DTCC board (which is made up of representatives of Wall Street brokerage firms) supported the proposal. I was incredulous. Apparently, the SEC's instinctive reaction was to be more concerned about what Wall Street brokers wanted than about the viability of the DTCC's solution and its desirability for investors and the market as a whole. At a later meeting with Ted and Senator Isakson, Isakson asked, "How long ago did DTCC develop this idea?" Larry told us it was more than a year ago. That meant that the DTCC had sat on it for months even before the SEC had sat on it.

We wanted the sitting to end. Within a month of hearing about the DTCC's idea, I'd helped Kaufman recruit seven other senators to write to the SEC endorsing the idea as a potential solution to abusive short selling. The letter was signed by Ted, Isakson, Levin, Jon Tester (D-MT), Sherrod Brown (D-OH), Orrin Hatch (R-UT), and Robert Menendez (D-NJ). Senator Arlen Specter (R-PA) wrote a follow-up letter concurring with it. Supremely confident (and a bit naïve), I said to Ted: "We're going to change the way stocks are traded in this country."

Not long after receiving the letter, the SEC announced it would hold a public roundtable to discuss naked short selling and possible solutions on September 24, 2009. I was convinced we were making progress.

We must have been. Because major banks like Goldman Sachs started lobbying furiously against any restrictions on short selling. The day before I was to meet with Goldman, an Isakson staffer told me that he'd received data from Goldman. "What did they say?" I asked. "That the data proves we're full of shit," he said. He sent it to me. It was bogus. Goldman had used market-wide data to demonstrate that there was no correlation between short selling and price movements. But a market-wide approach proved nothing about whether bear raids could succeed in driving down the price of a particular stock. I fired off an e-mail to Goldman's lobbyist, whom I knew well: "This use of data is so far beneath Goldman's reputation as to be laughable. To be meaningful, any correlation analysis should be in a single stock's shares around some event." I asked him why they didn't provide us with their own trading data in Lehman and Bear shares and added that he'd better not try to foist misleading data on us again.

During a conference call that same day, an exchange CEO tried to use the same misleading data on Ted, who replied: "Bring me facts, bring me something

I don't know. But bring me bullshit and I'll never forget." An exchange staffer called to tell me that the CEO
had been shocked; no one had ever talked to him that
way. From that day on, the word was out on Wall Street
that Ted was on the warpath. (I later learned from reporters that Wall Street was frustrated that they
couldn't find a way to harness Ted or pull his reins;
there was no obvious way to pressure Ted because he
wasn't running for reelection.)

To its roundtable the SEC had invited nine bank-
ing-industry participants, all but one of whom was in
favor of maintaining the status quo. During the meeting, the DTCC representative sat mute and didn't even
mention the DTCC's proposed solution for naked
short selling. Afterwards, I went over to Larry and Bill
and asked "What happened?" Sheepishly, and to their
credit, they admitted, "We got pulled back." They
meant: by their board, by the Wall Street powers-that-
be. It was just as the SEC staff had predicted (and even
encouraged) months before.

I said to Larry, "You'll be lucky if Ted and Senator
Isakson don't go to the Senate floor and flay the skin
off the DTCC." Afterwards, someone at the roundtable meeting told me he'd overheard Larry say privately to the Goldman Sachs member on the DTCC
board, "We're going to have a couple of senators
very upset with us but I think we'll be okay." I was
seething. In fact, by this time, Ted and I were both candidates for anger-management training, and Wall
Street would've been happy to pay for it. Even SEC

Chairman Schapiro had said at the roundtable: "It's interesting to me that an industry that is so technically adept at finding ways to make money cannot come up with a technical solution to naked short selling." I was the only Senate person in the audience who knew the DTCC *had* come up with a technical solution.

There were two reasons why Wall Street didn't want to adopt it. First, banks make an enormous amount of money lending stock for short sales, and so no big bank wanted to change the status quo. Second, and perhaps more importantly, stocks now traded in microseconds; millions of shares change hands (including in short-selling transactions) in the blink of an eye. High-frequency traders would oppose any solution, like the DTCC's, that required that shares be located and marked before being sold short. A high-frequency trade has no time to get its ticket stamped before jumping on its high-speed train.

After the roundtable, we decided to focus on exhorting the SEC to take action rather than making life difficult for Larry and Bill at the DTCC. After all, they had at least tried to do the right thing. The SEC had fostered the proliferation of trading venues. High-frequency traders now dominated these venues— sometimes to the detriment of ordinary investors. So far, the SEC hadn't done anything about it. Ted would spend the rest of his term trying to level the playing field for ordinary investors. And trying to get the SEC to do its job.

11:

THE RISE OF THE MACHINES

IN LATE AUGUST 2009, I was on vacation in Yellowstone, gazing at antelope and anxiously awaiting the publication of the next day's *Wall Street Journal*. I got up at 5:30 a.m. the next morning, eager to read my e-mails. But due to spotty wireless coverage, I had to walk out of the cabin and hold my BlackBerry aloft to retrieve them. They started pouring in as the *WSJ* article, "Senator Seeks Broad SEC Market Study," hit newsstands and cyberspace. In a letter to Chairman Schapiro, Ted had called on the SEC to review all forms of current stock market structure. The *WSJ* called the letter "the broadest statement yet from a legislator in the continuing debate over the growth in high-frequency trading, a lightning-fast, computer-based trading technique." Ted had landed his first punch in the fight to protect average investors.

Undeterred by our setbacks in seeking the return of the uptick rule and tighter restrictions on naked short selling, Ted and I had delved deeper into an even more arcane, complex, and problematic realm: the

overall functioning of the U.S. stock market. As MBAs
and experienced investors, we thought we knew how
the stock market worked. We didn't. Our knowledge
was dated; and with regard to ominous new develop-
ments, it was nonexistent.

I, like many people, still thought of stocks being
traded on an actual exchange (like the New York Stock
Exchange, or NYSE) or through a dealer-based system
(like the NASDAQ). But the SEC had adopted rules
that had resulted in the creation of scores of new exchanges and electronic trading platforms. The rule
changes were designed to end the NYSE-NASDAQ
duopoly, to increase the number of trading venues, to
promote competition between them, and, ultimately,
to reduce trading costs for investors. The result is a
highly fragmented market consisting of more than
sixty trading venues. To compete for market share,
these venues encourage or permit a number of practices that are potentially unfair to average investors.

One practice is referred to as dark pools. In dark
pools, big institutional investors trade large blocks of
shares with each other. Because these transactions are
private, they don't reveal big investors' trading strategies
to the broader (or, to continue the metaphor, "lit")
market. That's their attraction. Dark pools have flour-
ished. In 2004, there were eighteen dark pools comprising 1.5 percent of the market's volume. By 2009,
there were over fifty comprising 12 percent of the volume. Altogether, off-market trading—in dark pools or
internally at broker-dealers—accounts for nearly one

quarter of U.S. stock-trading volume. For retail investor orders, it may be twice that amount.

Another practice is high-frequency trading (HFT), which the *Economist* dubbed "The Rise of the Machines." HFT involves trading stocks on the basis of sophisticated computer algorithms capable of making trading decisions in microseconds. In conjunction with HFT, the proliferation of trading venues has created opportunities for the fastest and most sophisticated electronic traders to deploy profitable new trading strategies. This lightning speed enables these traders to stay microseconds ahead of many other investors and thus to lock in tiny, but relatively risk-free, profits. Repeating this process millions of times a day (sometimes with thousands of orders being placed every second) makes HFT a highly profitable business. Between 2004 and 2009, HFT had jumped from 30 percent to almost 70 percent of daily trading volume.

Our stock market had changed dramatically. No one understood how these changes were affecting average investors. Today's stock market is a constantly evolving, bewilderingly complex electronic labyrinth. Not even sophisticated traders can say with certainty what happens to their order when they buy or sell shares of stock. Ted's August 2009 letter to Schapiro publicly admonished the SEC for waiting too long to analyze the changes the market had undergone and urged it to get to work. Schapiro responded within a week, assuring us that the SEC would conduct a comprehensive study of the effects that market changes were having on average investors.

Ted's letter to Chairman Schapiro helped draw the media's attention to dark pools and HFT, which began to receive extensive (and concerned) coverage in the financial press. The letter also transformed Ted from a virtually unknown Senate newcomer into a brightly flashing blip on Wall Street's radar screen. In response, Wall Street scrambled an entire air wing of bankers and lobbyists to buzz Capitol Hill. Soon, squadrons were swooping into our office, anxious to thwart new regulations following the financial crisis and, particularly, to prevent a crackdown on HFT. They were numerous (we typically met with five high-level Wall Street executives at a time) and unanimous. Whether a megabank, broker-dealer, or a hedge fund, they all said they believed that the stock market had never functioned better. "Competition has driven down the costs of trading," said one. "The spread between a stock's asking price and offer price has never been so narrow," said another. "There's always enough liquidity—even during times of market stress—to ensure that trades will almost certainly be executed," said a third. The refrain "mom-and- pop investors have never had it so good" was intoned by nearly all of them. As a former lobbyist, I almost had to admire the way they unswervingly stayed on message. And the message was that the status quo was good for everyone and that Ted and I were wasting our time exploring whether market changes might call for statutory and regulatory changes.

It would've been easy, and quite understandable, for us to be convinced by Wall Street's unanimous message. But we'd been educating ourselves about these issues and we were convinced that there were, to use Donald Rumsfeld's locution, too many unknown unknowns for us to stop burrowing for answers and prodding the SEC. Our chief burrower was Josh Goldstein, a twenty-two-year-old college graduate who'd deferred entry to Yale Law School for a year to come work for Ted. Josh is brainy, curious, and tireless. He spent all day, every day, immersing himself in the arcana of HFT, stock market structure, and regulation. He soon became so knowledgeable that his questions in meetings would elicit who-the-hell-is-this-kid looks from Wall Street lobbyists. We also had help from a few industry insiders (who worked with us on the condition that we never mention their names publicly), which suggested there was less unanimity than Wall Street wanted us to believe.

We learned about a range of trading strategies, some of which are beneficial to the average investor, but some of which are predatory and harmful. One HFT strategy is called pinging. It involves attempting to "uncover how much an investor is willing to pay—or sell for—by sending out a stream of probing quotes that are swiftly cancelled until they elicit a response. The traders then buy or short the targeted stock ahead of the investor, offering it to them a fraction of a second later for a tidy profit" (the *Economist*). Another HFT strategy is called quote-stuffing. It involves purposefully sending millions of orders to one trading venue to slow it down imperceptibly so that the trader can take advantage of time and price disparities at other trading venues. There are also momentum strategies (in which traders take a position in a stock and then use HFT to generate market momentum that would benefit their position) and liquidity-detection strategies (in which traders use HFT to front-run—that is, buy or sell microseconds ahead of—incoming orders from pension and mutual funds). An SEC staffer stated that in some instances these strategies "could be manipulation" and "would concern us."

The Tabb Group estimated in 2009 that HFT generates $8 billion in profits annually. The question is: How much of this profit is from legitimate practices that benefits all investors, and how much of it is effectively an illicit toll extorted from average investors without their knowledge?

Other potentially questionable practices had been introduced by the trading venues themselves. The practices have strange-sounding names: flash orders, special data feeds, co-location services, and naked access. Their purpose is to enable a trading venue to draw HFT volume to itself (instead of to competing venues) in order to increase its revenues.

Flash orders made national news in July 2009, when the NYSE asked Senator Chuck Schumer (D-NY) to push the SEC to object to the use of flash orders by DirectEdge, a rival exchange. When Schumer did so, the *New York Times* ran a front-page story about it. Orders are supposed to be automatically routed to the trading venue with the best execution (in other words, the best price). But flash orders, the *Times* wrote, enable some high-speed traders to see other traders' orders before the rest of the market (and to take corresponding action, including holding the order for a period of time so favored customers might take it before rerouting the order to another venue, which might give them, not the orderer, the best price). Put simply, it was like one player at a poker table being able to see the other players' hole cards. It sounded like cheating.

Trading venues know that high-frequency traders want to receive information as quickly as possible. They cater to this desire by offering, for large fees, special data feeds and co-location. Special data feeds are custom-tailored in ways that assist (and thus reduce the processing time of) traders' complicated algorithmic strategies. Co-location simply means charging a trader to put his computer server directly next to the trading venues' own servers, which enables the trader to receive information a few milliseconds before the rest of the world. Because every millisecond—indeed, microsecond and, soon, nanosecond—is critical in HFT, traders are willing to pay millions of dollars annually for these advantages.

Trading venues were also offering high-frequency traders naked, or unsupervised, access to their trading platform without any requirement that brokers implement pre-trade risk controls on HFT activity. A study showed that as many as 35 percent of trades on exchanges were unsupervised. This meant that an offshore hedge fund in the Cayman Islands might be using manipulative trading strategies directly on a U. S. exchange.

Thanks to Josh's intrepid research and synthesis, tutorials from our covert industry insiders, and our own exhaustive (and exhausting) reading, Ted and I became extremely knowledgeable about these practices and how they affect market stability. In fact, Ted even predicted the flash crash—when the market dropped one thousand points in just minutes on May 6, 2010—eight months before it happened. In a speech on September 14, 2009, the anniversary of the collapse of Lehman Brothers, Ted warned of a flash crash and how HFT would fuel it:

> [U]nlike specialists and traditional market-makers that are regulated, some of these new high-frequency traders are unregulated, though they are acting in a market-maker capacity. They have no requirements to "maintain a fair and orderly" market. They trade when it benefits them. If we experience another shock to the financial system, will this new, and dominant, type of pseudo market maker act in the interest of the markets when we really need them? Will they step up and maintain a two-sided market, or will they simply shut off the machines and walk away? Even worse, will they seek even further profit and exacerbate the downside?

One problem we faced—and one you may be experiencing as you read this chapter—is that HFT isn't just mind-boggling. It's mind-numbing. Senator Kay Hagan (D-NC), a fellow freshman who'd become Ted's friend, was presiding in the chair on the day Ted gave the above speech. Ted told me afterward: "When I started, I saw she wanted so badly to listen and understand. After about five minutes I could tell I'd lost her." In each of the nine floor speeches on stock-market structure and HFT Ted would eventually give, our goal was to achieve a balance between technical detail and comprehensibility.

Helping other senators understand HFT, flash orders, and dark pools was one challenge. Another was to get them to care. In Washington, if an issue isn't in the newspapers, no senator is going to care much about it. So Ted and I worked the press aggressively and were rewarded. Articles about our crusade appeared in Bloomberg, Reuters, and the *New York Times* Deal-Book, where reporter Cyrus Sanati called Ted's letter to Chairman Schapiro "scathing." Reuters columnist Matthew Goldstein wrote, "The Delaware senator is taking the right approach in asking the Securities and Exchange Commission to conduct a broad review of HFT, so-called flash orders and dark pools. It's a much better approach than the more narrow one taken by Sen. Chuck Schumer, who last month focused solely on the impact of flash orders on the market." For a recognized expert to describe Ted as ahead of Schumer, one of the Senate's savviest members, on new, sophisticated financial issues was welcome recognition of our efforts.

In October 2009, about six weeks after his August letter to SEC Chairman Schapiro, Ted asked her for a meeting. When she walked into Ted's office, my first re-action was that I thought she looked exhausted, which made me feel some sympathy toward her. Ted had been spitting bullets at the SEC for months, but even his manner seemed to soften from meeting her and sensing her fatigue. After they exchanged pleasantries, Ted launched into a brief summation of his views, which he'd been using effectively with his fellow senators:

> Just like with derivatives, which blew up and nearly sank the country, we've got the same for-mula with HFT. I call it the Kaufman Formula. Whenever you've got a lot of change, a lot of money, no transparency, and therefore no effective regulation—watch out. Because the next thing you could hear is "boom." There's been a lot of change. The stock markets have transformed dramatically in only a few years time. There's a lot of money. The daily market volume by high-frequency traders is now over 60 percent. And they're making billions of dollars a year. There's no transparency. The SEC has admitted you're not collecting any data and you have almost no baseline understand-ing of HFT. And therefore we have a rapidly ex-panding market that's operating completely in the dark, with no effective regulation. I'm very worried that this is a prescription for another disaster.

Schapiro took it all in. She responded by reiterating her pledge, which she'd made publicly in response to Ted's letter, that the SEC would conduct a comprehensive review of market-structure issues and HFT. She added that she had many other issues on her plate. And indeed she had. America had just been through the biggest financial disaster in sixty years; Bernie Madoff's Ponzi scheme had gone undetected by the SEC for years despite repeated warnings from whistleblowers; investors were rattled and worried that the SEC was toothless. Nevertheless, it was obvious to me that she only had one choice if history was to judge her well: she had to *do* something.

Ted must have been thinking the same thing. Near the end of the meeting he told Schapiro, "I don't believe you're going to do anything about high-frequency trading." Looking him straight in the eye, she replied, "You just watch." We watched for nearly three years. It wasn't until July 2011 and June 2012 that the SEC approved minimalist rules that would force market participates to collect the data that would enable the SEC to begin—*begin*—the process of understanding HFT's impact on markets. In effect, Ted and I and America are still watching and waiting for the SEC to take meaningful action.

Back in the fall of 2009, the tone had now changed in our meetings with big Wall Street players. Fearing broad regulatory change, some players stopped telling us that nothing was wrong with America's stock markets. They begin admitting that specific practices—

usually their competitors'—were harmful. "If you think what I'm doing is interesting," they'd say, "let me tell you about these other guys." The broker-dealers complained about the exchanges, and the traditional exchanges complained about the upstart exchanges. We heard about illicit HFT practices that were disadvantageous to mutual and pension funds. After being buzzed by squadrons of Wall Street representatives, it was refreshing to have them drop supplies onto us instead. They seemed to have decided to work with us.

12:

THE FLASH CRASH

JUST AS SUDDENLY as they'd started, Wall Street's supply drops of information stopped. The financial industry would no longer talk to us. My interpretation was that our crusade was receiving too much publicity; Wall Street had decided that providing us with information would only make us more troublesome. They'd compete with one another in the marketplace, but not in the halls of Congress. From this point forward, any banks and securities dealers we could entice to meet with us went back to assuring us that nothing was wrong. The financial crisis had been caused by the credit markets; the stock markets have never worked better. They were back on message. And it was frustrating.

After several of these fruitless meetings, Ted changed the way he ran them. Instead of starting by presenting our concerns and having our guests respond, he invited them to talk. And let them talk and talk and talk. Josh and I wouldn't interrupt with questions or comments; we remained silent, encouraging our guests in the belief that they were achieving conviction. When a speaker had finally finished, Ted would ask, "So you don't think there are any problems or issues with the stock markets that should concern me?"

"No, Senator, we don't."

Then Ted would ask, "Do you think the SEC has started to collect any data about HFT practices?"

"Well, no," the guest would admit.

"Do you think your clients understand exactly what HFT is doing in every dark pool?"

"Eh, no," he admitted again.

"Do you think it's possible that some high-frequency traders are pinging orders with feints and cancellations and looking for ways to trade ahead or manipulate price? Do you think that's possible?"

"Well, yes," he admitted.

After more successful cross-examination on other issues, Ted would erupt: "Then why the hell didn't you start the meeting by saying all that? Why is it you people circle the wagons and won't let Congress ask reasonable questions?" The unexpected grilling and eruption never failed to make an impression. Seeing the discomfort on our guests' faces, I felt, I confess, a certain guilty pleasure.

Our top priority was to get the SEC to identify (or, to use the industry term: tag) high-frequency traders and collect data about their trades. Under current rules, such data weren't collected. So it's impossible to track an order as it wends its way—if "wend" can apply to a journey that takes a microsecond—through the electronic trading labyrinth and is executed. In fact, the entire reporting system for the execution of trades is antiquated. The SEC doesn't even monitor brokers to ensure they execute trades fairly. Oversight in this area has been outsourced to the Financial Industry Regulatory Authority (FINRA), of which Schapiro was the chairman and CEO from 2006 to 2008. A self-regulatory organization for broker-dealers, FINRA has often been criticized for being lax in policing the industry and generous in compensating its executives (Schapiro's regular compensation for 2008 was $3.5 million).

We met repeatedly with FINRA to learn what, if anything, it was doing to detect manipulation in today's microsecond trading environment. FINRA admitted to me that its computer programs only allowed it to monitor the market in multi-second increments. They were, in effect, engaged in the hopeless endeavor of using a Brownie camera to capture an image of a bullet train. "Guys," I said, "there's an entire multi-billion dollar industry of high-frequency traders operating within your margin of error." As it stood, no one could look for, or detect, stock manipulation at the current high speeds. FINRA didn't dispute this. For our part, we were determined to prove that a workable monitoring solution was possible. So we threw ourselves into composing another letter to the SEC. Attached was a five-page memorandum that detailed the obsolescence of the current reporting requirements and offered specific suggestions, gleaned from some of the top experts in the field, on how to update them.

Meanwhile, the pushback from Wall Street was intense and multi-pronged. The Blob oozed through the halls of government, seeking, through its glutinous embrace, to immobilize the legislative and regulatory apparatus, thereby preserving the status quo. The executive jets of the Wall Street air force flew sortie after sortie, transporting high-ranking emissaries from New York to Washington to meet with the SEC, Dodd and Shelby staff, and the staff of other senators on the Banking Committee. Some of the executives, no doubt less enthusiastically, even met with Josh and me. The research companies and market experts Wall Street employs also raised their voices against us. At times it got ugly. Ted was called a crackpot and dangerously uninformed. He was accused of "politicizing" market regulation (a strange notion considering he wasn't running for election). It seemed as if Wall Street, which wasn't used to someone on Capitol Hill asking in-depth questions about arcane issues, wished to silence or marginalize its critics. Industry people would always ask me, "What got Kaufman so interested in this stuff?" Used to politicians whose top priorities were to please their home-state business interests and raise money, they had trouble fathoming that Ted was so interested because it was the right thing to do. He believed in fair markets. And because he was genuinely concerned about emerging issues that threatened the stock market, where half of all Americans keep a sizable portion of their retirement savings.

On October 21, the SEC announced three proposed rules on dark pools. Cyrus Sanati of the *New*

York Times DealBook declared it a "win" for Ted and his repeated calls for action. But we believed the rules, which were supported by most of Wall Street, were incremental and inadequate. In our response we said: "Banning flash orders and imposing limits on dark pools should not be the end of the story, nor should they be seen as sacrificial lambs offered up by a substantial majority of Wall Street players as the price to ward off a deeper review." We wanted more action from the SEC. And from Congress.

Unfortunately, when it comes to oversight, Congress is a grandstanding, hectoring medical examiner rather than an attentive, foresightful physician. It ignores the patient's symptoms, acts surprised when that patient dies, and then turns the autopsy into a public spectacle. Not surprisingly, Congress waited until after the BP oil spill to put executives and regulators under oath (and in front of TV cameras) and make them explain themselves; before that, it had been content to assume that everything was dandy and to soak up campaign contributions from the oil industry. To be honest, Ted's hearings and meetings about financial-crisis-related fraud constituted yet another congressional postmortem, this time to prod the Justice Department into aggressively investigating the Wall Street executives whose malfeasance had helped kill the economy. With HFT and market-structure issues, however, we wanted to demonstrate how Congress could conduct effective real-time oversight of emerging problems—and not wait until the next Depression.

It's fair to ask what the Senate's chief overseer of the financial industry and its regulators—Chris Dodd (D-CT), chairman of the Banking Committee—was doing as the financial crisis approached; that is, when treating the patient, not just dissecting the corpse, still would've been possible. Much of the time, it turns out, he was in Iowa running for president. In 2007, as the subprime lending crisis was unfolding (it was to hit with full force in 2008), Dodd held just four Banking Committee hearings on issues that were at least somewhat related to the growing threat: predatory lending practices (February 7); mortgage-market turmoil (March 22); the modernization of Fannie Mae and Freddie Mac (July 18), whose collapse fifteen months later would cost taxpayers hundreds of billions of dollars; and the impact of credit-rating agencies on subprime credit (September 27). Obviously, these hearings didn't forefend the financial crisis. And, to be fair, it's possible that not even the most skilled diagnosticians would've been able to detect, and prescribe the right treatment for, America's diseased mortgage industry. But it's also possible that more aggressive congressional oversight could've saved America billions of dollars.

The Banking Committee's hearing on HFT, held in October 2009, was decidedly not an example of aggressive oversight. The witnesses were seven industry representatives, James Brigagliano (who was then the acting director of the SEC's Division of Trading and Markets), and Ted. Senator Bob Corker (R-TN) summed up the committee's seeming insouciance when he said, "It sounds like everything is all right to me." Ted, who'd been the sole witness on the first panel at the hearing, was the only senator to do any follow-up.

He wrote a letter to the SEC on November 20, highlighting the SEC's testimony at the hearing about possible manipulation and pressing it to provide a timetable for three areas. First, when would it finalize a rule that prevents high-frequency traders from having unsupervised access to trading venues and that requires brokers market-wide to implement pre-trade risk controls on HFT? Second, when would it finalize a rule that requires brokers to collect data on large high-frequency traders (which would finally give the SEC baseline information about how high-frequency traders operate)? Third, when would it require a consolidated audit trail (which would fill the gaps in reporting requirements that prevent the efficient tracking and policing of orders and trades)? The third issue was crucial. A consolidated audit trail would give the SEC eyes. Without it, the SEC can't see what's happening and therefore can't stop manipulative trading strategies, detect disruptive rogue algorithms, or reduce excessive market volatility. (By July of 2012, almost three years later, all three rules have finally been adopted.)

As the months wore on, we continued to pester the SEC, to no avail. I'd e-mail an SEC staffer: "It's been 111 days since Chairman Schapiro said she'd propose a rule to collect data on HFT. What's taking so long?" They'd reply with a list of I's that needed to be dotted and T's that needed to be crossed before they could take action. After waiting some more I'd write again: "When I talked to you 45 days ago you said it was coming soon." If my tenure as Ted's chief of staff taught me anything, it's that the C in SEC doesn't stand for the speed of light.

And then came May 6, 2010. That day, at 2:40 p.m., the Dow Jones took a dizzying thousand-point plunge in minutes and just as quickly rebounded. Some stocks that had been trading at $45 a share were suddenly trading for a penny. On air, Jim Cramer of CNBC's *Mad Money* watched Procter & Gamble plummet and said to his viewers, "This is crazy, you gotta buy at these prices." The event, which soon became know as the flash crash, eviscerated investor confidence and awoke the entire world to the dangers of markets dominated by computer trading.

As an investor, I was terrified. I called my broker: "What happened?" He didn't have a clue. As Ted's chief of staff, I was jubilant. It would vindicate Ted during his time in office and show that Wall Street (and The Blob) had been in denial. Only days earlier, on April 30, the Security Dealer Association had written to the SEC: "Equity markets are functioning properly, and there are no signs of significant deficiencies or an inability to perform their important functions." Ted was the one man in Congress who'd tried repeatedly to warn the financial industry, its regulators, and his colleagues before it was too late.

As the market gyrated dizzily, one of Ted's colleagues, Senator Mark Warner (D-VA), remembered the warnings. Warner's chief of staff, Luke Albee, called and told me "the senator wants to talk to Kaufman *now*." At that moment, however, Ted was essentially incommunicado. He was in the Senate chamber, taking his two-hour turn as the presiding officer. While presiding, he couldn't answer his cell phone and could only rarely sneak a peak at his BlackBerry. Luke told his boss where Ted was, and Warner went straight to the Senate floor. I watched on C-SPAN as he walked up to the presiding officer's chair, spoke briefly with Ted, and then descended to the well. "The chair recognizes the senator from Virginia," Ted said.

"I rise to talk about what happened in the market today," Warner started. "While it closed down 347 points, at one point it approached a loss of 1,000 points, which would have been the largest single day loss in modern history." Initial reports suggested that it had been caused by a "technology glitch." This is an area of "expertise of the presiding officer," Warner continued, referring to Ted, adding that "I have heard my friend come to this floor time and again to talk about the challenges that have been created in the marketplace" by computer-driven trading. "We may have seen the first inkling today of what happens when these tools don't work the way [they're intended]." He concluded his remarks by saying that "[w]e at least need to have more facts, as today was a living, breathing, real-time example of the potential catastrophe that can take place." Then he turned, looked at Ted, and said, "I have become a believer."

Ted had become the Oracle of Delaware, the man who'd read the algorithmic auguries of high-frequency trading and foreseen the flash crash. Jim Cramer of *Mad Money* called Ted the "most sophisticated man in Washington" and someone who was looking out for the average investor. Ted's clairvoyance gave him instant credibility with many of his colleagues, and we intended to use it. I immediately started drafting a letter from Ted and Warner to Chris Dodd. We delivered it the next day, May 7. The letter asked Dodd to add to the Wall Street reform bill then before the Senate the requirement that the SEC and the Commodity Futures Trading Commission (CFTC) conduct a joint study of what had caused the flash crash and how it should be dealt with. "A temporary $1 trillion drop in market value is an unacceptable consequence of a software glitch," the letter said. "We are concerned that, as markets rely on and entrust such a high percentage of the capital management of the market to black-box trading that systems systemic problems may be created." The Kaufman-Warner amendment would've directed the SEC and CFTC to report to Congress on a variety of specific questions and possible solutions within a specified number of days of the reform bill's enactment.

This was our vision of effective, foresightful Congressional oversight. Congress should help the regulatory agencies identify the most pressing problems, assign the problems the urgency they deserve, and suggest possible improvements. But the Kaufman-Warner amendment was ignored. I met with a Dodd staffer and agreed to a number of modifications (requested by the Dodd staffer, that is, before he'd even bothered showing it to his boss). Dodd announced that the Banking Committee would hold a series of hearings. But there was only one hearing. And then, nothing.

The SEC, for its part, did slightly more than nothing. In collaboration with the stock exchanges and FINRA, it devised and implemented market-wide circuit breakers that, it hoped, would significantly narrow the amplitude of any future crashes. But it still had no real knowledge about how HFT strategies affected the market or the average investor. As CNBC's Jim Cramer later said of the SEC, "The lifeguard is off duty. And when you go swimming in this market, you'd better remember there's nobody out there making sure the water is safe."

The flash crash taught at least three lessons, all of which Ted had identified long before May 6, 2010.

First, stock prices don't always reflect the market's best estimation of the value of the underlying companies; in mini flash crashes, they can result from the breakdown of algorithmic trading strategies.

Second, technology has far outpaced regulation. Regulators' lack of understanding of HFT strategies and the volatility they create left the markets vulnerable to a nausea-inducing plunge. For example, the SEC took for granted that high-frequency traders were the new market makers without taking into account the ways in which they differed from traditional market makers. Not only did the speed of HFT algorithms cripple the markets in a matter of minutes, but the absence of true market makers to guarantee two-sided markets in times of high volatility created an enormous liquidity shortage. Andrew Haldane, executive director for financial stability for the Bank of England, said that the flash crash demonstrates that HFT is "adding liquidity during a monsoon and absorbing it during a drought." Although circuit breakers may make a crash less calamitous, they're not a cure for regulatory ignorance.

Third, the lack of data made identifying the causes of the flash crash a monumental task. It took armies of SEC and CFTC staffers more than three months to painstakingly recreate the trading activity of that one twenty-minute span. This indicates how far the agencies are from being able to monitor trading activity in real time.

Newton's first law of motion states that "every object continues in its state of rest, or of uniform motion in a straight line, unless compelled to change that state by external forces acted upon it." If he'd replaced "object" with "organ of government" he'd have written the first law of organizational inertia. Ted and I knew all about that law, because we felt its immobilizing force every day on Capitol Hill. So we knew how difficult it was for an organization like the SEC to think, and move, in new ways (particularly with the weight of The Blob serving as a constant check against motion). We tried to be a helpful, not hectoring, external force, to prod with useful ideas, not jab with invective. As the Reverend Jesse Jackson might have said: we tried to engage, not enrage. During his term in office, Ted went to the floor every week to praise a federal employee. One week, he picked an SEC employee, an attorney in the Enforcement Division who'd recently won an insider-trading case involving U.S. treasury bonds. The speech was an opportunity to reassure SEC employees that one of their toughest critics was nonetheless sympathetic to their situation. "As the SEC embarks on its next chapter, I want all of its employees to know when they walk out of that lobby each day and see the Capitol dome, they should feel confident that those of us who work under it are their partners. . . . The era of looking the other way is now behind us. The time has come to look forward."

It was, in keeping with Ted's character, a noble sentiment and heartfelt (as trite and corny as they may sound, I believe those modifiers aptly capture Ted's intent). On the other hand, we were well aware of the three main impediments to the SEC taking meaningful action. First, nearly all the data, evidence, and analysis the SEC uses to monitor the financial industry come from the industry itself, creating a temptation for the industry to spin the data in its favor (as we'd seen with the naked-short-selling data provided by Goldman Sachs). Second, The Blob oozes endlessly in and out of the revolving door of public service. According to the Project on Government Oversight, 219 former SEC staff members filed 789 "postemployment statements indicating their intent to represent an outside client before the commission" between 2006 and 2010. In other words, 219 former government officials were representing Wall Street clients on matters before the SEC. Third, because the SEC has been so slow to start collecting data about HFT, it's still years away from being able to propose HFT regulatory rules that it can empirically justify based on hard data (as the federal courts will require it to do).

Attached to our final letter to Chairman Schapiro, dated August 5, 2010, were eight pages of proposals for addressing the above-mentioned (and other) shortcomings: the need to bring light to dark pools, to eliminate conflicts of interest, to ensure that regulators have the data they need to prevent manipulation and accurately assess whether small investors are being ripped off. The letter pointed out that how the SEC responds to our proposals is "a test of whether [it] is just a 'regulator by consensus,' which only moves forward when it finds solutions favored by large constituencies on Wall Street, or if it indeed exists to serve a broader mission."

As part of our effort to engage, not enrage, we didn't drop the letter through the SEC's transom like a hand grenade and run away. Prior to August 5, I met with the director of the SEC's Division of Trading and Markets and provided him and his deputy with an hour-long briefing on everything we'd learned and what the letter would propose. As a joke and gesture of good will, I'd taken along a Senate calendar with the prior days X'd off and a big red circle around Ted's last day in office to indicate that we suspected they were counting the days. Ted had signed it and added "Keep up the good work!" After I finished my presentation, one of the director's responses was, "Wow, it's great to hear from someone who isn't from the industry." When I got back to my office, I called a friend who'd been a top staffer for former SEC Chairman Bill Donaldson, and he told me, "Jeff, it's true. The only people who walk through the SEC's door are Wall Street people bitching about SEC proposals."

The reaction of the financial press to the August 5 letter was overwhelmingly positive. Gillian Tett of the *Financial Times,* who devoted an entire column to the letter, said, "Kaufman's ideas definitely deserve to be widely aired." Jeremy Grant of the *Financial Times* wrote that same day that Ted turned "some impressive diagnosis of what's wrong with market structures into some pretty bold and counterintuitive proposals of his own." A week later, the *Financial Times* ran an editorial entitled, "Taming Trading," which said: "Mr. Kaufman is right to raise a bigger question: who is served by ever-deeper liquidity? Equity markets in particular are not the mere playground of traders, but a place where retail investors deploy their savings. As regulators catch up with reality, they must ensure markets serve the non-professional users who access them." Neil Lipshultz, editor of the Dow Jones Newswire, also devoted an entire column to Ted's efforts, writing that "besides showing an acute understanding of the myriad and obscure workings of today's stock trading—dark pools, high-frequency trading, excessive messaging and the like—Kaufman has eight pages of proposals." As *Zero-Hedge*, a prominent pro-investor blog, wrote: "Ted Kaufman shows everyone how it's done."

In December 2011, after Ted had left the Senate, the SEC's Market Abuse Unit invited him to speak to a large gathering of its employees. The speech was broadcast throughout the SEC. Dan Hawke, director of the unit, introduced Ted. He said that our August 5 letter to Chairman Schapiro had provided the outline the unit had used for all of its work since then. He went on to say that it was the best statement of the market-structure issues and best road map for dealing with the problems that they've found. He said it demonstrated how knowledgeable the Kaufman Senate office had been on these issues from the beginning. For us, Hawke's remarks were gracious recognition that our real-time, foresightful approach to oversight was helping to guide at least one arm of the SEC.

13:

WATERLOO

IN MAY 2001, Senator Jim Jeffords of Vermont left
the Republican Party, declared himself an independent,
and started caucusing with the Democrats. This gave
the Democrats a one-vote majority in the Senate,
which meant that Biden became chairman of the Foreign Relations Committee, a position he'd long cov-
eted. At about this time, Ted and Dennis asked
whether Jack and I would hold a big Biden fundraising
event at Quinn Gillespie. The event was a huge success.
It raised over $75,000 for Biden and was a well-timed
celebration of his ascendance to foreign relations chairman. I introduced him and told a story from 1979 of
the *Tuscaloosa News* editor defending his decision—to
me, an irate college student—to banish to the back
pages Biden's revelation that Soviet troops in Cuba was
a phony issue because Biden's speech was "only one
man's opinion." Now, I said, that opinion carries
weight around the world.

Jack and I hosted a similar event for Biden two
years later. Biden, whose assistant campaign treasurer
had embezzled $350,000 of campaign funds, showed

almost maudlin appreciation to the crowd for helping refill his coffers. As usual, he didn't thank me, either at the event or afterwards, even though I'd done more work than anyone to make it a success. This time, I couldn't remain silent. When Dennis took me to lunch to thank me for the event, I told him that not only had Biden let me down at a critical moment of my career (by not calling Mikva), he couldn't seem to bring himself to thank me when I bust my ass to help his political career. It had been more than twenty years since Biden had signed my notebook "Please stay involved in politics, we need you all." I had—but had received precious little from Biden in return. As a lobbyist, I'd not once asked for a meeting with or favor from Biden (to his credit, he was famous for not doing them anyway). A little personal appreciation wouldn't kill him. Though taken aback, Dennis was sympathetic. After all, for the past twenty years, he, like Ted, had been mollifying the many dissatisfied members of the extended Biden family.

Two weeks later, I received a handwritten note from Biden: "Jeff, you've always been there for me. I hope you know that I will always be there for you." This, after "thanks for being a true friend," was the second disingenuous note Biden had sent me. He'd never been there for me, not in any direct way that had propelled my career or raised my standing in Washington. All he did—weeks after the fact, presumably after succumbing to pressure from Dennis—was send me one-line notes.

Yet I consciously decided to keep playing along and

advised every other former Biden staffer to do the same. It was in our interest to stay involved with Biden. I called it the New Contract. Yes, Biden was an equal-opportunity disappointer; he wouldn't lift a finger to help anyone but his family, a tiny group of insiders, and his longtime backers in Delaware. But Ted and Dennis will always help. Biden is only getting more powerful in DC. Do the math, I'd say (to them and myself): It makes sense to be known across Washington as a Biden guy in good standing. No one needs to know the truth. Besides, while I'd become increasingly disappointed by him personally, he still had the strengths as a politician I'd admired when I first met him: his command of the issues (those he cared about), his positions on most issues, and his occasional will-ingness to buck party orthodoxy to do what he thought was right.

That was my line in 2004 when I roped in as many Biden supporters as possible to raise money for John Kerry's presidential campaign by holding a George-town cocktail party at which Biden and the late Richard Holbrooke had agreed to speak. We printed invitations saying Biden and Holbrooke would be there. By working the foreign policy establishment hard, we raised more than $200,000. On the day of the event, I got a call from Biden's scheduler, asking me if I would hold for Biden. He came on the phone: "Hey, buddy. How badly do you need me to be there tonight? I really want to go home to Delaware." I couldn't believe he was trying to back out. "Senator, there are going to be 150 people there tonight who wrote $1,000 or more checks because I promised them you'd be there. You simply have to keep your word to me and show up." Biden grudgingly said he would.

Like supplicants for ambassadorial posts, droves of Professional Democrats had attended, hoping for their one-on-one moment with Biden and Holbrooke. Professional Democrats are not just the lobbyists. The term applies to almost all Democrats in the legal, policy, foreign policy, and even national security worlds, each of whom is trying to climb the greasy pole of power. Currently, Clinton veterans are Washington's dominant generation of Professional Democrats. Professional Democrats don't shake up the system; they *are* the system, and they want to preserve it so that it works best for them. They want to serve at least a year or two in every Democratic administration as part of their steady rise in the Democratic hierarchy. That night, many of them had made the maximum allowable contribution to the Kerry-Edwards DNC account.

Not every former Biden staffer bought into the New Contract. Five of the seven friends from the 1987 Biden campaign with whom I still had lunch once a month had stopped helping Biden. Even though I was disappointed, I did my best to keep the flame alive among former staff. I still wanted to believe that I— the college student who'd met Biden and later left Wall Street to join him—was symbolic of Biden's ability to inspire people, to change lives, and to lead. If he could do it with me, he could it with other people.

In truth, by this point none of us believed that Biden had a realistic chance of becoming president. But the New Contract—to those of us who upheld it in its strongest form—included playing along with Biden's presidential delusions. So when Ted asked me in 2006 whether I wanted to be involved in the upcoming Biden presidential campaign, I said "sure." Why quit now? In the one-in-a-thousand chance that Biden struck lightning in Iowa, the payoff on all the chips I'd put on the table over the years could be huge. It was like Pascal's wager. I should live as though God exists and Biden will become president, because in both cases I have everything to gain and nothing to lose.

Because I'd raised more money for Biden in Washington than anyone else in the past fifteen years, Ted asked me to be treasurer of Biden's new political action committee, Unite Our States. Our inaugural fundraising event in Georgetown raised $200,000 (and I actually got a thank-you voicemail from Biden). Ted also once again got me involved in the early campaign strategy sessions. The first I attended with Biden was at his house in Wilmington. It was a gathering of his biggest rainmakers, people who'd raised money for him over the years or who were proven fundraisers who'd expressed support for him this time around.

Most candidates make hundreds of calls a day. In contrast, when it comes to fundraising, Biden (and Ted) are products of their home state, which is tiny. If you throw a party in Delaware, you'd better invite everyone—or no one. If you only invite a few people, the rest of the state will hear about it and be angry that they were left out. The same thing applied, so went the Biden campaign logic, to personal calls from the senator: if he calls some people, everyone will expect a call and be disappointed if they don't get one. That's why Biden always had his disciples pass the hat for him.

More importantly, Biden absolutely hated making fundraising calls, and everyone at the meeting in Wilmington knew it. Biden said to us: "I'll challenge you on how much time I should spend doing fundraising, because I believe momentum is more important. If I can generate a rise in my poll numbers in Iowa, that will do more to raise money than if I spend all day on the phones when I'm stuck at 1 percent. But once we jointly decide on a strategy, and we reach a compact on how much of my time should be spent doing calls, I give you my word I'll do them." Later in the campaign, a twenty-three-year-old fundraising staffer got into a car with Biden with a list of names and phone numbers: "Okay, Senator, time to do some fundraising calls." Biden looked at him and said, "Get the fuck out of the car." At moments like this, even I could be an enabler. Instead of confronting Biden with his churlish treatment of a kid who was just following instructions, I went into mollify-mode and tried to make the staffer laugh: "How fast was the car moving at the time? Did you do the tuck and roll that I taught you?"

In a town preoccupied with fundraising, Biden was indeed an exception. Other senators typically spend hours out of every day calling big fish to do events for them or even smaller donors for $1,000 contributions. Harry Reid, the Senate majority leader, when given a long list, has called past Democratic contributors who didn't even know who Reid was when they took the call. Delaware, which is the size of a large county in most other states, had spoiled Biden. He liked keeping his integrity intact; fundraising, he perceived, was a threat to it and one he'd long avoided. Presidential campaigns are gigantically expensive cash-raising contests, and he was ill prepared for it.

If Biden lacked the discipline necessary for a presidential campaign, so did, this time around, his inner circle. None of the stalwarts wanted to work on the campaign full-time, and they were having a hard time finding a campaign manager and other campaign staff who'd devote eighty hours a week to the campaign. Biden's bid, which pundits unanimously considered hopeless, nearly ended before it started. The day he announced his run for president, an interview surfaced in which he'd called Barack Obama "articulate and bright and clean." He'd actually been trying to be complimentary, but his adjectives sounded condescending and, in the case of "clean," at least latently racist.

Because of my history with Biden in Texas, I made a point of flying to Houston for a fundraiser organized by many of the same people who had done events for Biden in 1987. Over the years, I'd become friends with two of them, Greg Jones and Ron Franklin. The Houston event was at Greg's home. Biden arrived and began speaking to a packed living room. Dinner was waiting in the next room, but Biden was just getting started. As a longtime staffer, I knew to keep flexing my knees while standing through a Biden speech. After awhile, I noticed that the room was getting uncomfortably warm. Suddenly, a woman fainted. Two men caught her and carried her out a side door. Biden just kept on speaking. Finally, Dennis had to come in and announce that dinner was getting cold. As the guests filed into the dining room, I stood in the foyer and asked a couple of them for their impressions. "He's got senatorial disease," one said. "He talks too much." At that moment, the front door opened, and the foyer was bathed in the flashing red lights of the ambulance into which the fainting victim was being loaded.

On this campaign, Biden and I saw more of each other than we usually did. Before one event, we were alone together. I did what I always did: put on a fake smile, said how good it was to see him again, and briefed him on the group he was about to speak to. This one time, Biden apparently tried to get past what had happened between us. He gave me a quizzical look, as if to ask, "Why are you like that with me? Why aren't we friends?" He even started to say, hesitantly: "Why are you, why can't we . . . ?" I looked at him and didn't say anything. Maybe another time, I thought, because we aren't going to solve a decade of bad feeling in the three seconds before the host walks through that door to start this event.

In September 2007, I went to Iowa to get a feel for the campaign. It was the weekend of the Harkin Steak

Fry, an important political rally hosted by Senator Tom Harkin that draws all the of the candidates and thousands of Iowans. On the Saturday before the Steak Fry, I spent the day with Danny O'Brien, Biden's former chief of staff, who now served as the campaign's political director. Danny would spend a year of his life in Iowa, living out of a suitcase, putting in eighty-hour weeks, and making one of the greatest personal sacrifices for Biden I'd ever seen. We went to the Iowa-Iowa State football game, and Danny worked the state senators and representatives he hoped would endorse Biden. We also went to a backyard Democratic barbeque, where Biden's son Hunter shook hands and joked with everyone there. At both events, we ran into Senator Chris Dodd, whose campaign was even more quixotic than ours, but with whom the Biden people (even I) shared a sense of incredulity and injustice that upstarts like Barack Obama and Hillary Clinton were getting more traction than experienced hands like Biden and Dodd.

Driving to the Steak Fry the next day, I saw scores of buses filled with Obama and Clinton supporters; as I got closer, hundreds of people in Obama and Clinton T-shirts were streaming to the event. Not a single Biden sign or supporter. The event itself was like an outdoor rock concert, with thousands of people spread across a hill, looking down on the stage where the candidates would speak. The crowd seemed to be evenly split between Obama and Clinton, with a sprinkling of Richardson and Edwards supporters. I turned to see

Biden and a few staffers entering the grounds. I went up to Annie Tomasini, Biden's deputy press secretary, and asked her where our supporters were. As Biden, undaunted, waded into the crowd and started pressing the flesh, Annie said, "We're hoping for a snowball effect."

The hope went unanswered. Biden did well in the televised debates (famously responding with the single word "yes" to the question "do you have the discipline not to talk too much?"), but his poll numbers were mired in single digits. So our fundraising never improved, and we operated on a shoestring. Meanwhile, Obama was raising tens of millions of dollars. After the 2008 campaign, statistics would show that three of the top seven employers of Obama's largest contributors were Goldman Sachs, J. P. Morgan, and Citigroup.

In early December, I flew to Iowa to stay (except for a brief holiday break) through the caucuses, which were scheduled for January 8, 2008. After watching the final debate in Des Moines, my plan was to travel with Biden for a couple days to get a sense of his message and how he was connecting with caucus voters. The next day started early with a breakfast in a supporter's home in southeast Iowa. There were about forty people there. Biden put his arm around, and chatted briefly with, each one of them before he was introduced to speak. His speech wasn't very good. He spent a lot of time on his résumé. A question about climate change sparked a change, though. He gave a passionate answer, talking about his early involvement with the issue as a sponsor of the first fuel-efficiency bill. Okay, that's more like it, I thought.

Our next stop was a small hall in Fort Madison, and Biden was warmed up now. He walked among the thirty people who'd shown up, extemporizing a speech that had a clear narrative line and that wove in, at the proper moment, genuinely funny stories from his many years in the Senate. It was an outstanding performance and vintage Biden. If he didn't just convince those people he should be president, I thought, he never will. Biden tried to give the same speech at the next stop, but this time it was disjointed, and at one point he told the punch line to a story without having set it up. It was clear that Biden had done little or no preparation and was trying to wing it at every stop. Sometimes he pulled it off, sometimes he didn't.

Having seen enough to realize we weren't going to win, I drove on to Waterloo. The Waterloo headquarters were dingy and depressing, but the staff was young and enthusiastic. Greg Jones had come up from Houston to ride out the campaign with me. His wife later joined us. It was tough work doing the phone banking and door-to-door canvassing, just as I had for Biden for so many years in his Senate campaigns. Each night, we went to a casino outside Waterloo for a nice dinner and a glass of wine, dulling the pain of the slow march toward caucus-day disaster.

Each icy Iowa morning, Greg and I met for breakfast or a workout at the local gym before starting another day of drudgery. I'd bought a GPS for my rental car so I could find my way around the area. At night, as I drove through snow-covered farmland to another tiny town to drop off campaign supplies, the GPS only rarely had to issue instructions. It simply displayed a straight pink line across a dark, empty screen. I was counting the days until that pink line had run its course, and I could get back to my life in Washington.

14:

BATTLING THE
MEGABANKS

TED AND I OCCASIONALLY made the rounds in New York City, not only to meet with stock exchange and Wall Street executives, but also to visit key members of the financial media. We'd start in New Jersey at CNBC, where Ted sometimes would co-host *Squawk Box* or appear on Jim Cramer's *Mad Money.* Then we'd head to the *New York Times* and meet with prominent financial journalists like Andrew Ross Sorkin, Gretchen Morgenson, and Louise Story. At the *Wall Street Journal,* we developed relationships with Scott Patterson and Geoff Rogow, who routinely broke interesting stories about stock trading. And we'd go to Bloomberg and Reuters, which also had leading financial reporters who were shaping the public's views on Wall Street regulatory issues. We wanted these reporters and columnists to call Ted often as a go-to source for quotes.

On January 15, 2010, Ted and I were in New York and met with Paul Volcker, the legendary former Federal Reserve chairman, to talk about Wall Street reform. After Obama's election, Volcker had been marginalized as an economic advisor but was still an advocate for strong financial reform. As Robert Kuttner of the *American Prospect* has written, "Volcker was a menace because he was counseling more constraints on bank powers than Summers and Geithner wanted. It speaks volumes about this administration that the most radical person in the room on the subject of banking reform was usually the former chairman of the Federal Reserve." Former chairman Volcker received us graciously, stooped at the shoulders but still standing almost to his full six feet, seven inches in height then ushered us into his conference room. Volcker began, "You know, just about whatever anyone proposes, no matter what it is, the banks will come out and claim that it will restrict credit and harm the economy . . ." He took a long pause while Ted and I leaned in closer to hear what he'd say next.

"It's all bullshit." Ted and I laughed. We were relieved . . . and emboldened. Volcker outlined his idea for banning banks from engaging in high-risk proprietary trading. After 1999, when Congress repealed Glass-Steagall (the 1933 Depression-era law that separated commercial banks with their federally insured deposits from investment houses), banks with federally insured deposits had started trading for their own accounts, using excessive leverage and making risky bets, implicitly relying on a federal safety net to catch them if they failed. That needed to end, Volcker said.

Ted said he wanted to go further. In December, Ted had become an original co-sponsor of a bill introduced by Senator Maria Cantwell (D-WA) and former GOP presidential nominee Senator John McCain (R-AZ), to reinstate Glass-Steagall. Ted believed Congress had made a mistake in repealing it (indeed, long before 1999, the Federal Reserve had adopted rules—several over Volcker's objection—that had begun to tear down Glass-Steagall's limits). That led to a wave of financial-sector consolidation and the creation and growth of megabanks. Ted said Congress should restore what it had enacted in the 1930s and what had worked so well for so long to preserve financial stability (until first the Fed and then Congress unwisely dismantled it). Volcker said cagily, "Well I won't stand in the way of someone who wants to do something more dramatic." Volcker knew having Ted and others further out on the reform flank would make his own proposal seem like a comparatively centrist idea. As a strategic matter, Ted agreed. By being for Glass-Steagall, he could at least run interference for Volcker.

The next week, I was tipped off that President Obama would announce, in the wake of Scott Brown's victory in the special election for the late Ted Kennedy's Senate seat in Massachusetts, his support for legislation to impose a so-called Volcker Rule, exactly what Volcker had described to us the previous week. I immediately went to work on a speech, which Ted delivered on January 21, 2010, the same day as the president's announcement, applauding the Volcker Rule and calling on the Senate to enact strong Wall Street reforms. In that speech, Ted laid out his views. He blamed Congress for repealing Glass-Steagall, thereby bringing to an end an era of responsible banking regulation and the beginning of an emerging laissez-faire consensus that markets could do no wrong. Over the past decade, inaction allowed derivatives markets to remain unregulated (even after the Fed had to orchestrate a multi-billion-dollar bailout of a hedge fund, Long Term Capital Management, which had used derivatives to leverage a relatively small amount of capital into trillions of dollars of exposure). The Fed and other banking regulators had ignored widespread instances of predatory lending and deteriorating standards for mortgage-origination. The Fed had been slow to write consumer protection rules. Bank regulators had relied on credit ratings and banks' own internal analytical models when determining the amount of capital banks must hold. Moreover, regulators had essentially permitted banks to park the worst of their activities off their balance sheets at non-bank affiliates or entities created for this purpose. Finally, the multifarious bank regulatory agencies were poorly coordinated and badly captured by the industry. "Perhaps most importantly," Ted stated, "this era of lax regulation allowed a small cadre of Wall Street firms to grow completely unchecked, without any regard to their size or the risks they took."

It leaked from the White House that Biden had helped push President Obama to support the Volcker Rule; a faction in the White House apparently believed, belatedly, that Obama must at least be viewed by the voters as tougher on the banks. Maybe Ted's activism was beginning to have an effect, through Biden, on Obama's thinking. Ted even quoted Biden in his Volcker speech: "As Vice President Biden aptly and succinctly put it: 'Be a bank or be a hedge fund. But don't be a bank hedge fund.'" I was happy but skeptical. I knew Ted talked to the vice president, but Ted never told me about the substance of those conversations. Those stayed forever in Ted's vault. That's one of the reasons Biden trusted him so much.

That speech was the first time Ted used the phrase "too big to fail"—as recently popularized by Andrew Ross Sorkin's book, which sat on Ted's desk. In the next six months, he would practically wear it out, urging the Senate repeatedly to deal effectively with too-big-to-fail megabanks before they caused yet another disastrous financial crisis.

On a subsequent trip to New York, we met with Bill Dudley, the former chief economist at Goldman Sachs who is president of the New York Fed. Dudley was clear about what he believed needed to be done. In the past, he said, bank regulators had failed to require banks to hold sufficient capital reserves and had let these same investment banks and banks use too much short-term leverage. In the future, he continued, regulators can correct the problem by increasing capital and other regulatory requirements in proportion to bank size and interconnectedness. The largest of the megabanks would face the highest capital ratio requirement, providing the necessary incentive to restrain growth or even shrink.

It all sounded very simple and straightforward. Just one problem, Ted said. What if two or six or ten or fourteen years from now we have a new president, one who is deeply conservative or even libertarian? What if that new president appoints regulators who, just like those of the Alan Greenspan era, don't believe in bank regulation? The pendulum may eventually (or even fairly soon) swing back to laissez-faire. As the shock wears off from the last crisis, Ted added, regulators may again become captive of politically powerful mega-banks (they are today). Congress, Ted believed, must write clear statutory lines; otherwise, Dudley was asking Ted to trust the wisdom of future regulators, when neither Dudley nor Ted could even predict who those regulators will be. Dudley answered, as we'd predicted he would, by saying that bank capital requirements must be coordinated internationally with other nations' regulators. We're on it, he said. To Ted and me, that sounded too much like Congress had little to no role. His answer dodged Ted's central point about future presidents appointing regulators Ted couldn't know (and wouldn't trust).

Back in the Senate, Ted had three great insights. First, this wasn't a time for vague legislation that kicks the can back to the very regulators who'd failed in the lead-up to the crisis; Congress needed to draw hard statutory lines, just as it had during the Great Depression. Second, Wall Street's inherent conflicts of interest had to be resolved through structural reform, such as by reinstating Glass-Steagall or imposing size and leverage limits. Third, he wanted to take the fight straight to the megabanks on too-big-to-fail, making Wall Street defend against structural reforms it opposed, at least to increase the chance that other provisions opposed by the banks, like the Consumer Financial Protection Bureau, would pass.

It's true that Bear Stearns, Lehman Brothers, Merrill Lynch, and Goldman Sachs had all operated without a bank charter during the crisis—and had been at the center of it. But due to their extensive derivatives holdings, the risk of these non-bank institutions failing had become a threat to the entire financial system, and those that didn't fail subsequently had sought bank charters and substantial Fed assistance. Ted believed that Congress needed to strike directly at the heart of the structural problems on Wall Street. Volcker's proposal was at least a step in that direction. But Ted thought Congress should place strict limits on the size, leverage, and trading activities of behemoth financial institutions (both banks and non-banks).

In the fall of 2009, Chairman Dodd had begun drafting a proposed Democratic bill that built on a previous Treasury-White House proposal. On the issue of too-big-to-fail, the bill established a Financial Stability Oversight Council (presumably to foresee emerging systemic risks, but in reality not likely to be better at predicting the future than the existing President's Working Group on Financial Markets); provided enhanced Fed supervision for banks and non-banks deemed to be systemically significant (in reality, the

Fed already had such power); established so-called resolution authority, which would empower the FDIC to
take over and resolve a failing institution (ignoring the
reality that megabanks are global and U.S. authority
stops at our borders); and tightened regulation of derivatives trading. The bill also called for the creation of
a consumer financial protection bureau and contained
myriad other provisions.

After months of drafting, Dodd presented it to the
Banking Committee on November 19, 2009. It was a
1,139-page proposal, and the committee's ranking
member, Senator Richard Shelby (R-AL), lambasted it.
He ripped into Dodd and the committee for not having developed an "exhaustive factual record" of what
had caused the financial crisis. Then he labeled the
draft bill a failure, one that would require a "complete
rewrite" before it might gain Republican support. In
particular, Shelby criticized the bill for institutionaliz-
ing the notion of too-big-to-fail—by creating a category of banks and non-banks deemed to be
systemically significant—rather than ending it. On
that issue, Shelby's critique was similar to Ted's (though
Shelby proffered no alternative solution).

Dodd went back to the drawing board. He empowered four bipartisan pairs of Banking Committee members to work on different parts of the bill. Then, he
began a closed-door negotiation seeking bipartisan consensus. For weeks and then months, quiet talks dragged
on between Dodd and the Republicans. The House of
Representatives had passed its bill in December 2009,

but in the Senate, for months thereafter, there was no message, no bill, and no floor debate. Time crept by without a single senator saying anything publicly about Wall Street reform. At the same time, no Wall Street prosecutions were forthcoming from the Justice Department. To me, given that the country had been crippled by a devastating financial crisis, this long period of silence in its capital seemed bizarre.

Not coincidentally, it was during these months when the Tea Party, strongly opposed to the strenuous efforts of Obama and Congressional Democrats to pass a healthcare bill, grew deep roots. In my view, the Senate had waited far too long to turn to Wall Street reform. Frankly, I wasn't that interested in healthcare reform and was surprised and disappointed that the Senate spent so much time on it. I didn't know the issues, I had little to no confidence that the bill would do what its sponsors claimed it would do, and I was far more concerned about the health of the economy and pursuing Wall Street. To me, it didn't feel like the right time to spend almost a year crafting major healthcare legislation. Ted believed strongly in passing healthcare reform. He also kept saying he wanted to be a "good soldier" for the president. He'd go to the floor repeatedly and make passionate arguments. I'd listen and bite my tongue.

Regardless, I attended an early July 2009 session when top White House aides David Axelrod and Jim Messina came to meet with the Democratic chiefs of staff about the urgency of passing healthcare. That

morning, as usual, I'd watched CNBC's *Squawk Box.*
The recovering Dow had slipped from 8,736 on June
10 to 8,132 on July 10. It looked like the economic recovery was losing traction. I knew that millions of
investors were deeply worried (I was sweating about
my own portfolio) and that millions of others were still
out of work.

Yet here were the president's top emissaries and they
weren't talking about jobs or the economy. Messina
said, "We talked to the president last night. And he
said, 'You know, I spent two years running for president. I visited all fifty states. I must have personally
talked to two million Americans. And I want to give
them healthcare reform.'" I thought, Obama may have
spent two years running for president, but he'd won
the election because the financial crisis hit and the
economy went over a cliff. Shouldn't we first fix a broken Wall Street and American economy? That was my
rather nasty train of thought, that morning. I lacked
the guts to say it out loud. The second message came
from Axelrod: "And you need to pass healthcare before
the August recess." I was thunderstruck. Does anyone
think that can happen that fast with something this
complicated? Again, I wish I'd had the guts to say it.
But this was the belly of the healthcare reform beast.
Many of the people in the room had lived the dream
of healthcare for all Americans for much of their
careers. And, most importantly, Ted was a staunch
supporter of passing healthcare.

I *had* spoken up once before. In April 2009, a

White House communications staffer came to the Senate to talk about the healthcare message. He summed up nicely the three main points: Under the reform bill we'll *cut costs; if you like your doctor, you can keep him;* and all Americans will receive *quality, affordable healthcare.* The White House had just held an event with executives from the pharmaceutical, health insurance, and other industries, at which this coalition announced it would favor healthcare reforms that cut costs in the coming decade by $2 trillion. That weekend, the editorial page of the *Washington Post* had been dubious about the event's lack of detail on precisely how to cut the $2 trillion. So I raised my hand and asked the White House staffer about the editorial. His response: Yes, at some point we'll have to worry about that. But weren't the optics great? All these groups that used to oppose healthcare were now in favor of it. About a month later the Congressional Budget Office scored the first version of the Democratic healthcare bill. According to CBO, the first draft of the bill would *cost* taxpayers $1.6 trillion, not save $2 trillion. I immediately predicted (incorrectly) that healthcare reform was doomed.

Across America, people were still hurting and angry. And so the public's anger directed itself at the Democrats, who were perceived as putting healthcare reform and the trillions it would cost (even if offset in the end by revenue raisers) over the need for economic recovery. And frankly I couldn't blame them. I sat through too many meetings where dozens of issues were discussed but never the need for programs to create jobs and ensure economic recovery. Obama and the Democrats had taken their eyes off the ball. It erupted that August, when the Tea Party movement, already under way, had harshly criticized Democrats at town hall meetings. The three Republicans who'd been negotiating a healthcare bill with Democratic Senator Max Baucus—Chuck Grassley (R-IA), Mike Enzi (R-WY), and Olympia Snowe (R-ME)—came back with fear in their eyes and pulled out of negotiations.

In September, the Democrats—furious with Baucus for having wasted so much time with Republicans who clearly weren't negotiating in good faith—were still in denial. Harry Reid took over the process and unveiled a healthcare plan that included a public option, even though he knew it would never pass. Reid was up for reelection and needed to appeal to the Democratic base. That caused months more of delay. It seemed like the Democrats and Obama were obsessed with healthcare reform when the rest of America was obsessed with jobs and economic recovery. Meanwhile, Wall Street reform, which Americans favored by wide margins, languished.

After the surprising win by Republican Scott Brown in Massachusetts and the Democrats' loss of a 60-vote majority, many Democratic senators began to argue that the Democratic message must focus on two things: jobs and Wall Street reform. That, they believed, was our way back. The Democratic caucus seemed to have gotten the message, as Majority Leader

Reid moved directly to a jobs bill. It was fruitless to negotiate with Republicans, many Democratic senators
believed, because since the previous August (and, indeed, earlier than that) the Republicans had adopted a
strategy of opposing everything. Even if the Democrats
made concessions to Republicans in committee, the
Republicans would filibuster the bill on the Senate
floor.

When Senate Finance Committee Chairman Max
Baucus nevertheless produced a jobs bill that he'd negotiated with Republicans, including tax extenders and
other miscellaneous goodies for Corporate America,
Ted reported that the Democratic caucus revolted. Senator Sherrod Brown (D-OH) stood up to say he was
appalled that he'd first heard about the bill's provisions
from lobbyists on K Street (many of Baucus's former
staff work downtown). The Democrats directed the
Majority Leader to strip those items from the bill,
frame a strong jobs message around the bill, take it to
the Senate floor, and dare the Republicans to filibuster
and vote against it. The strategy worked. Five Republican Senators crossed the floor and voted with the Democrats, giving them the sixty-plus margin to break
the filibuster and pass the bill.

It seemed obvious to Ted and me that that same approach should be the strategy for the Wall Street reform
bill. The Republican caucus, carrying Wall Street's
water, would never give in. We needed a strong bill, a
strong message, and a campaign to achieve broad public support. Polls showed that 67 percent of Republican

voters believed Congress needed to "enact rules to rein in Wall Street excesses." The same polls showed that the public believed, by two-to-one, that Obama Democrats favored the interests of Wall Street over Main Street. Only a strong reform bill and effective message campaign could turn around that negative perception, strong enough to compel four or five Republican Senators to cross the aisle and break a filibuster.

Dodd's negotiations dragged on longer. Still, Ted didn't expect to be a leader in the battle, whenever it finally came. Senators Cantwell and McCain had their Glass-Steagall bill. We expected Senator Jeff Merkley (a bright fellow freshman Democrat from Oregon) to be a leading pro-reform voice on the Banking Committee. In 1999, Senator Byron Dorgan (D-ND) had fought valiantly against the repeal of Glass-Steagall. And Senator Carl Levin (D-MI) would soon make his mark with his series of hearings in the Permanent Subcommittee on Investigations. We waited for other reformers to sound the battle cry. I prodded Cantwell's and Merkley's staffs especially to seize the opportunity for their bosses, they'd be heroes to millions of Americans. Weeks and months crept by, and Dodd still kept trying to give away provisions to gain Republican votes in committee. Cantwell went months without doing anything. Merkley decided to cooperate in the Banking Committee, so he didn't take the lead until after the committee reported a bill and he and Senator Levin introduced their version of the Volcker Rule. And Byron Dorgan only belatedly began to take the lead.

Impatient for Senator Cantwell to move forward on her Glass-Steagall amendment, Ted and I went to see her. She had two staffers with her, and Ted and I sat down on her plaid silk couch. The meeting started, and Ted couldn't hold back. He kept telling Senator Cantwell everything he had learned, all that he thought. How bad the Republicans were. How big the banks had gotten. How Washington had let the Depression-era laws crumble and fall, leading to disaster. I was beginning to get uncomfortable. Ted, who just a year ago had been determined not to get "senatorial disease," barely stopped to take a breath. Finally Senator Cantwell interjected, "Ted, we need to get you more excited about this issue."

Cantwell didn't say it, but I suspected one of her problems was that Senator McCain, her amendment co-author, was facing a tough primary fight in Arizona. In a heated battle for Tea Party voters, no Republican could be perceived to be cooperating with a Democrat, so McCain had probably retreated from his initial enthusiasm. Ted finally let Senator Cantwell provide her views, but after that meeting, nothing ever came of the Cantwell-McCain amendment. Cantwell's excuse to Ted later was that she couldn't find any supporters beyond the usual reform-minded senators; apparently, because so many of the sitting Democratic senators had voted in 1999 to repeal Glass-Steagall, few wanted to admit they'd made a disastrous mistake.

Dodd continued to negotiate with Shelby, making concessions to the Republican side. After weeks of taking Republican ideas into the bill, the Banking Committee held a mark-up to consider the bill. Shelby again blasted the bill up one side and down the other. Publicly, Dodd tried to laugh this off. But it was becoming increasingly clear to his Senate colleagues that Dodd was using the Republicans to negotiate with himself, apparently because he wanted to give his Wall Street patrons the weakest bill that would pass. This time, at a meeting of the Democratic chiefs of staff, I spoke out. I was loud and emphatic: "Stop negotiating with Senator Shelby. He's just a stand-in for Wall Street. Take a strong bill with a strong message to the floor. Americans want strong Wall Street reforms." Yet the chiefs for other Democratic senators on the Banking Committee repeatedly said, "We'll never get a bill that way. It has to be bipartisan."

"Why?" I kept asking. Apparently some of the Democrats on the Banking Committee (not just Dodd) wanted a bipartisan bill, too. They were fantasizing if they thought the Republicans would ever support a bill, but they preferred to tell Wall Street that gaining Republican support was essential—code, in effect, for ending with a weaker bill.

Ted was speaking out at caucus meetings. When Democratic political operatives recommended to the caucus that its message be Democrats are "on your side," Ted stood up to say: "I learned in politics a long time ago that people expect you to be what you say you are. Say you're smart, you'd better be smart. Say you're honest, be honest. If you say 'on your side,' you'd better be on their side. That can't just be a slogan, it needs to be a test of the bill's substance."

I was getting increasingly incensed and frustrated, so I started attacking Dodd on background in the press. For example, on March 15, CNBC ran a story quoting me as a Senate aide:

> Finally, there is concern that Dodd had drifted too far from key party positions on some issues in trying to find common ground.
>
> "Dodd should be moving a strong bill with a well-orchestrated campaign and message behind it, calling the Republican bluff," said another source, a senior Senate aide. "My understanding is that Dodd is moving forward with a bill that includes concessions. I thought you made concessions to gain someone's support. After four months of negotiations, Dodd has made concessions to get Republicans to consider it. I truly don't get it."

At a subsequent meeting of the democratic chiefs, pollster Stan Greenberg, whom the chiefs had invited to make a presentation, undermined my repeated suggestions about the best political strategy. While the healthcare reform bill remained stalled, Greenberg told the chiefs he believed it would be best if the Senate passed any Wall Street reform bill (even a weak one) if just to prove they were capable of governing, rather than taking a strong stand against Wall Street and risk more gridlock. My frustration nearly boiled over. Healthcare reform isn't popular; Wall Street reform is. If we take a strong stand against Wall Street, we'll pass a bill. We should be most concerned about what voters will think in November, especially if the Democratic base believes that the Obama-Democrat version of Wall Street reform is weak.

I still didn't know what was happening in the Banking Committee, where, it seemed, the negotiations were intense, secretive, and virtually round-the-clock. I called Jack Quinn and said, "I can't get to the Banking Committee. I assume you guys are having a hard time getting information about the bill negotiations?" To my surprise, Jack replied, "Actually, I spent forty-five minutes yesterday with Chris Dodd." He and the CEO of a client, which was concerned about provisions in the bill affecting systemically large non-banks, had a face-to-face meeting with Dodd, while I worked in the Senate and couldn't get a scrap of information. I e-mailed one of my fellow Democratic chiefs: "I came into government to help shape change on Wall Street, and now I realize the profession I just left is having more input on the bill than I'm having from inside the Senate." The chief responded, "That's really sad."

Ted had had enough. He was determined to go to the Senate floor and start speaking out strongly. I began working on a major speech. We wanted to lay out Ted's views on the importance of ending too-big-to-fail. He wanted it to be the foundational document (a favorite Biden tactic) for all he would argue during the debate.

We went through several drafts. Simon Johnson, the former chief economist for the International Monetary Fund and leading critic of too-big-to-fail megabanks, was standing by to tout the speech in his blog and on *Huffington Post,* where he served as a senior contributor. It took us longer than I'd planned. At one point, I e-mailed Simon: "This is threatening to become the speech that ate the Senator."

I wanted it to read like a long-form essay, because I knew few people would hear it when Ted delivered it to an empty Senate chamber (unless casting a vote, senators are rarely on the Senate floor, usually leaving any speaker to talk solely to the presiding officer and C-SPAN cameras). Finally, Ted and I were comfortable with our magnum opus. And so on March 11, 2010, just a day after he signed onto the Merkley-Levin bill to restrict proprietary trading, Ted delivered his longest speech yet: "Wall Street Reform that Will Prevent the Next Financial Crisis." It weighed in at 3,391 words (and that's the shorter version Ted read on the floor; the longer version, at 6,572 words, was placed into the Congressional Record).

It was, as Simon put it that morning in a *HuffPo* "splash" above Ted's picture, which filled my computer screen, "The Speech for Which We Have All Been Waiting." Simon wrote, "We need a simple speech and a direct speech, most of all a political speech—about what exactly happened to our financial system, and therefore to our economy, and what we must do to make sure it can never happen again."

The speech pulled no punches: "We are still far short of addressing some of the fundamental problems—particularly that of 'too big to fail'—that caused the last crisis and already have planted the seeds for the next one. And this is happening after months of careful deliberation and negotiations." The speech laid out a history of Wall Street, the "edifice" of regulations built during the Great Depression whose "protections and standards" were "methodically" removed, and a host of other factors which led to the 2008 crisis: the emergence of megabanks; the rise of shadow banking; the over-the-counter derivatives market; the expanding safety net; and the newer, more concentrated power of banks. Then Ted asked a "simple question": After a financial crisis that devastated America, triggered a Great Recession, and necessitated a $2.5 trillion bailout (counting Fed loans, too), "Why should those of us who propose going back to the proven statutory and regulatory ideas of the past bear the burden of proof? The burden of proof should be upon those who would only tinker at the edges of our current system."

The speech took the Dodd bill apart, noting the insufficiency of its resolution authority: "We need to break up these institutions before they fail, not stand by with a plan waiting to catch them when they do fail." Ted described the bill's banking provisions as reorganizing powers that regulators already possessed:

> They could have sounded the alarm bells and restricted this behavior, but they did not. They

could have raised capital requirements, but instead farmed out this function to credit rating agencies and the banks themselves. They could have imposed consumer-related protections sooner and to a greater degree, but they did not. The sad reality is that regulators had substantial powers, but chose to abdicate their responsibilities.

In short, the speech was an argument against incremental approaches; Ted proposed the need for radical surgery. Congress should draw hard lines: first, to rebuild the wall between the government-guaranteed part of the financial system and those investment banks that would remain free (within certain limits) to take on greater risk; and second, to put limits on the size, riskiness, and interconnectedness of systemically significant banks and non-banks. I sat there all morning watching Ted's huge picture on *Huffington Post*, as e-mails started to roll in from across the Senate and downtown. "Wow."

Just a week later, Arianna Huffington and two *HuffPo* reporters sat down with Ted in his Senate hideaway office for an interview. Six hours later, she posted an equally positive profile of Ted in her own column, headlined, "Celebrating Ted Kaufman, Accidental Leader" and leading with: "At a time when our political and financial landscapes are littered with villains and those unwilling to take them on, it's refreshing to find someone in the halls of power that we can unabashedly celebrate. Enter Sen. Ted Kaufman of

Delaware." Arianna drew heavily on Ted's views on too-big-to-fail and the rule of law, as this was also the week Ted had blasted government prosecutors for failing to charge Lehman Brothers executives for fraud and balance sheet manipulation. She wrote of his having delivered two "blistering speeches" in a week's time, noting that Ted had emerged as "one of the Senate's fiercest critics of Wall Street." She also held up Ted as an example of what the political system would produce if we took money and fundraising out of the equation. Ted winced when he saw that, and he always denied that he had more courage to take on Wall Street than most of his colleagues because he never had to raise money. "I'd be doing the same thing if I were running for reelection," he said to the press, over and over.

I never believed it. Ted never had to raise a single dime to get to office or stay there longer. That meant we didn't have to begin our day—like other senators and their chiefs of staffs start practically every Tuesday, Wednesday, and Thursday morning—by going to a fundraiser breakfast, where Wall Street lobbyists would've chastised us for not working with Dodd. Other senators and their chiefs spend part of their day fielding phone calls from bundlers who raised big dollars for their campaigns. Or they spend hours placing calls to others asking for fundraising help. They agree to meet with bundlers who provided analyses of why this provision would harm credit and that provision would somehow hold back economic recovery. And these same chiefs might be worrying about their next job, just as I had years ago.

As a former lobbyist, I can remember talking to senators about an issue and seeing the wheels in their brains turning quickly: How will this affect my race? It may be a money issue, a vote issue, or both. And every two years when I went into the field to help a senator up for reelection, I remembered why senators had to think that way. If he or she was up against a well-funded opponent, every dollar spent on every ad counted.

Ted, on the other hand, was free to let his punches fly. So Arianna and Simon set out to raise Ted's profile. In a reform movement, you need heroes. You need a narrative, with a hero who speaks the truth and bad guys who try to foil him. If Ted Kaufman hadn't existed, Arianna and Simon would have had to invent him.

On March 22, the Dodd bill was voted out of the Banking Committee, with no Republican or Democratic amendments considered. No one on the committee as yet wanted his or her differences to be known publicly. Ted decided to denounce it on the Senate floor. We worked together on a nearly four-thousand-word speech, which included his most pointed criticism yet. It was a withering critique, straight from the shoulder. When we finished the draft, I asked him: "Are you sure? This is really going to piss off Dodd and the administration." Without a hint of self-importance or exaggeration, Ted said: "I'm speaking to the ages." In part, he said:

What walls will this bill erect? None. On what bedrock does this bill rest if the nation is to hope for another sixty years of financial stability? Better and smarter regulators, plain and simple. No great statutory walls, no hard divisions or limits on regulatory discretion; only a reshuffled set of regulatory powers that already exist. Remember, it was the regulators who abdicated their responsibilities and helped cause the crisis.

After his speech, Ted took the chair to preside over the Senate, and Dodd took to the floor to talk about his bill. To the casual C-SPAN viewer, it appeared that Dodd had likely heard Ted's critique. The televised juxtaposition was striking, and Simon Johnson's banner posting that day leading *Huffington Post* used this headline, clearly referring to Dodd: "Senator, Which Part of 'Too Big to Fail' Do You Not Understand?"

More media attention followed. On April 1, *Yahoo*'s Aaron Task did a piece on Ted; that same day, the *New York Times* editorialized on too-big-to-fail (and mentioned Ted); on April 2, an interview with Ted by Benjamin Sarlin appeared in the *Daily Beast*; on April 6, *Newsweek*'s Michael Hirsh weighed in with a Kaufman profile; and, two days later, Reuters' Thomas Ferraro published his Kaufman profile. On April 8, Michael Scherer in *Time* wrote:

Instead of sailing quietly into oblivion, Kaufman has decided to make waves. Most notably,

he is challenging his Senate colleagues—and the
Obama administration—to get behind far
tougher financial regulations than they have yet
proposed, a move that has been unsettling to both
bank lobbyists and White House aides.

Ted was clearly upsetting the Democratic strategy,
which was to make the Republicans look like they were
against any Wall Street reform, while the Democrats
were for effective reforms. As Scherer wrote in *Time*,
Ted was saying the emperor has no clothes:

> As politics, his critique threatens to under-
> mine the White House's finely tuned election-
> year story line. To hear President Obama or his
> aides tell it, the coming Senate debate on financial
> regulatory reform will offer a clear choice to vot-
> ers this fall between most Democrats who are de-
> fending the interests of Main Street and most
> Republicans who are in the pocket of Wall Street.
> Kaufman, by contrast, argues that neither party
> has yet shown much seriousness about undoing
> decades of deregulation, and non-regulation, that
> created the conditions for the financial collapse
> in the first place. "Little in these reforms is really
> new," Kaufman says of the current White House-
> backed Democratic Banking Committee plan.

As he traveled around Delaware on the weekends,
Ted perceived a change among voters. At a Common

Cause dinner, he walked in and got a standing ovation. People in the hardware store would say, "Keep going after Wall Street!" He was pumped. He'd clearly struck a chord with a considerable portion of the state, although the banks (and Delaware's political class) were very unhappy with him. One of Delaware's top state officials visited me and castigated Ted for making Delaware look unfriendly to banks and business, which are crucial to its economy. Biden himself had been known among liberal critics as the senator from MBNA, at one time the largest credit card bank in Delaware and which had hired Biden's son Hunter. Biden had been a leading proponent of a bankruptcy reform bill that had been favored by the credit card banks, a large employer in Delaware. I even used to hear complaints about that from Iowa voters. Now, Ted, Biden's closest confidant, was campaigning daily against the interests of Wall Street banks (a different breed of cat than the smaller Delaware banks, which didn't like Ted for it regardless). And while Ted would never admit it, I could tell (from hearing Ted's half of phone conversations) that Biden secretly was cheering for Ted (the unleashed id to Biden's ego).

Most unhappy was Chris Dodd. In April during a congressional recess, he called Ted from Central America and left him a voicemail: "Stop saying bad things about my bill." Before returning Dodd's call, Ted asked me to call Ed Silverman, Dodd's staff director on the Banking Committee. Ted suggested I ask Ed in a nice way exactly how Ted can be for the changes he wants to the bill without being critical of it. "Ed, help me fig-ure this out. How does Kaufman do that?" With Dodd trying to muzzle Ted, it was a smart strategy.

I didn't know Ed and wondered whether he'd even take my call. But his receptionist and then his assistant, doubtless aware of Ted's blistering speeches, put me right through to him. I said my lines. Ed said, "Oh, that's just Chris feeling a little stretched. You guys are obviously free to keep saying whatever you want about the bill. I actually think you're helping Chris because now he can say he's got the Right and the Left upset with him, so he must be striking the right balance." I pressed Ed on why Dodd kept negotiating with the Re-publicans: "It makes no sense; you're just weakening the bill without picking up any votes." Ed replied, "From the beginning Chris has wanted a bipartisan bill." As our conversation ended, Ed said, "Don't worry about being critical. Chris will be the one who gets to take the victory lap in the end."

Ted was happy when I reported back. He wanted to maintain his friendship with Dodd (in part because Biden and Dodd are good friends and grew even closer during their ill-fated presidential bids). Then Dodd called Ted again, this time from Argentina: "I have a good bill. Will you please stop criticizing it." Perhaps my call to Ed hadn't worked after all. Ted told Dodd his bill didn't end too-big-to-fail. When Dodd re-turned, Dodd talked to Ted again on April 13 and 14, with both of them repeating their positions. Ted stressed that he'd never said anything personally critical of Dodd, but that they had legitimate and important substantive differences. Ted ended by saying, "Let's agree to disagree." (Months later, during Dodd's victory lap, he said in an interview, "It got pretty tense with people I like" and named a few Democratic senators, starting with Ted.)

I knew Dodd wanted to run over Ted like a speed bump. I was happy we were making life tougher for Dodd who, according to lobbyists I knew, was telling K Street that he'd be happy to throw some of the toughest provisions out of the bill, but that he couldn't because Democratic senators in his own caucus had him pinned down. Ted's flanking move was keeping a weak bill marginally stronger.

By mid-April, Ted's was no longer the sole voice. Merkley and Levin had gotten excited about their Volcker Rule amendment. They also began to host meetings of progressive Democratic senators who thought Dodd's bill was too weak. Dick Durbin (D-IL) tried to coordinate the input of senators who were dissatisfied with the Dodd bill. Al Franken (D-MN) had developed an amendment on credit rating agencies and conflicts of interest. Dorgan began pushing for a ban on naked credit default swaps (when speculators take a short position on a bond without owning the bond itself).

Blanche Lincoln (D-AR), the chair of the Agriculture Committee, which has jurisdiction over derivatives (futures markets originally existed to hedge commodities, especially agricultural commodities), had first

worked out a compromise with the committee's ranking Republican, Senator Saxby Chambliss (R-GA).
Then she suddenly reversed herself and authored a
much stronger derivatives-reform provision. For those
following the action closely, Lincoln's flip-flop was a
particularly egregious political calculation. Lincoln had
circulated a draft provision she'd negotiated with her
Republican counterpart, which pleased Wall Street,
then abruptly lurched to the left by authoring a much
stronger approach. Because Arkansas's lieutenant governor had challenged her in the Democratic primary,
she seemed anxious to please the Democratic base. Was
this the beginning of an anti-Wall Street political movement or just an Arkansas anomaly?

Cantwell suddenly came to life because she thought
Dodd was being disrespectful of Blanche Lincoln (a fe-
male colleague). She reportedly stood up in the Democratic caucus and said as much. Harry Reid and Dodd
backed down in a hurry. Lincoln's derivatives provision
went in the base bill. Dodd would just have to figure
out a way to water it down in conference. (He did, with
the acquiescence of Blanche Lincoln, who by then had
won her primary and was cynically moving back to the
right for the general election, which she lost.)

Senator Sherrod Brown (D-OH), who serves on
the Banking Committee, had called Ted after his
March 21 speech, and our two offices began collabo-
rating to develop an amendment based on the ideas in
Ted's floor speeches. The Brown-Kaufman amendment
to break up the megabanks became a rallying cry for

reformers. The assets of the six largest U.S. banks, which just fifteen years before had equaled 17 percent of GDP, had grown in size to total almost two-thirds of the American economy. The biggest banks had concentrated far too much financial risk (and political power).

Called the Safe Banking Act of 2010, the Brown-Kaufman amendment would have put limits on the size of and leverage used by megabanks by:

- imposing a strict 10 percent cap on any bank-holding company's share of the United States' total insured deposits;
- limiting the size of non-deposit liabilities at financial institutions (to 2 percent of U.S. GDP for banks, and 3 percent of GDP for non-bank institutions);
- setting into law a 6 percent leverage limit for bank holding companies and selected nonbank financial institutions.

We believed Brown-Kaufman was a more direct and simple way of achieving the goals of the Volcker Rule, which has subsequently proved difficult to define by regulation (and, eventually, enforce). Ted argued that the megabanks rely heavily on short-term financing like repos, trading liabilities, and commercial paper to finance their own inventories of securities, as well as their own book of repurchase agreements, which they provide to hedge funds through their prime brokerage business. The growth of those funding markets in the run-up to the crisis had been staggering. One report by researchers at the Bank of International Settlements estimated that the size of the overall repo market in the United States, the U.K., and the euro zone totaled approximately $11 trillion at the end of 2007. Incredibly, that was almost $5 trillion more than the total value of domestic bank deposits at that time, which was less than $7 trillion. The overreliance on such wholesale financing made the entire financial system vulnerable to a bank run, as during the Great Depression (before we instituted a system of deposit insurance and strong bank supervision). Remarkably, although there is a prudential cap on the amount of deposits the largest banks can hold, nothing limits bank liabilities like repos, which often must be rolled over every day. Brown-Kaufman would correct that problem by placing restrictions on the size of these liabilities at both bank and non-bank financial institutions.

Ted and Senator Brown argued that it's particularly critical we impose such limits now that the federal safety net has been expanded to cover not just traditional commercial banking franchises, but also investment banks engaged primarily in speculative activities. Prior to the financial crisis, investment banks, by gorging on wholesale liabilities like repurchase agreements and commercial paper, were able to forty-times leverage a small base of capital into asset holdings that, in some cases, exceeded $1 trillion. With the purchase of Bear Stearns by J. P. Morgan Chase (with financial support

from the government), the acquisition of Merrill Lynch
by Bank of America (allegedly under pressure from the
federal government), and the special dispensations that
Goldman Sachs and Morgan Stanley had received from
the Federal Reserve, all of the main Wall Street firms
are now either part of bank holding companies or have
become one themselves. Financial institutions whose
deposits are federally insured and which enjoy permanent access to the Fed window should stick primarily
to the business of banking. In short, Brown-Kaufman
would force the largest megabanks to break apart.

I'd hoped that Ted could convince Biden to work
within the White House to gain support for the
Brown-Kaufman provision and try to convince President Obama to embrace effective structural reform.
But considering the number of technocratic regulators
in the Treasury Department, Fed, and economic team
at the White House, that would have been a miracle.

As for the Treasury Department and Federal Reserve, Ted now really had their attention. The regulators and their fellow ideologues in the Obama
administration were determined to stop Congress from
drawing any hard lines. From the beginning, Treasury
wanted no legislation that would tie its hands in negotiating international capital standards. I thought that
was the height of technocratic arrogance. These people,
who had been over-deferential to the banks before the
disaster, didn't want anyone—certainly not any legislator who might represent millions of Americans who
had been crushed by the fallout—telling them what to

do. I started telling reporters that passing an empty bill (one that simply reshuffled existing bank regulatory powers) would be tantamount to following an abdication of regulatory responsibility with an abdication of democratic responsibility. In the 1930s, Congress drew hard lines, and it worked. During the age of regulatory flexibility and international capital standards, disaster struck.

I continued to worry that Dodd would reach a deal any day. A *Newsweek* story quoted me as a senior Senate aide: "We're gonna wake up one day, tomorrow or two weeks from tomorrow, and there's going to be a deal between Dodd and the Banking Committee Republicans, and that will be the end of reform. One can only hope the president realizes what's at stake." The article was entitled "Oh, Barack, Where Art Thou? With the president AWOL, a too-quick return to normalcy could scuttle financial reform." More than a year later, Frank Rich, in his first column for *New York* magazine after leaving the *New York Times,* wrote a stunningly fierce piece entitled "Obama's Original Sin: The president's failure to demand a reckoning from the moneyed interests who brought the economy down has cursed his first term, and could prevent a second." Obama, in my view, deserves that kind of criticism. Everyone in the White House during this period told me Obama was deferring to Geithner. Biden, I later learned, wasn't a factor. It was all in the Treasury Department. Obama, after insisting on a Consumer Protection Financial Bureau and having made his half-hearted move in favor of the Volcker

Rule, had gone back to the sidelines. The rest would be decided in brutal power politics—and we know who had the muscle.

And where was Harry Reid? He was running for reelection in a tight race, so I asked one of his staffers: "How is Reid using the Wall Street issue in his campaign? It should be helping his reelection to favor a tough bill." And what did I hear back? "He's already raised so much money from Wall Street that he's in no position to use it as a campaign issue." Indeed, the money was coming in so fast from Wall Street's coffers that someone asked Reid's campaign staff: "Shouldn't we talk about this from a campaign strategy perspective?" Nope, the answer came back. "Money is money."

Dick Durbin, who at one point had said, "The banks own this place," was number two in the Democratic leadership. Yet even Durbin said publicly that breaking up the banks was probably a "bridge too far."

15:

STILL TOO BIG TO FAIL

TED KEPT MAKING WAVES, and some washed over onto the major Sunday talk shows. On the April 4 edition of *This Week,* ABC's Jake Tapper played a clip from Ted's March 26 floor speech for his guest, Larry Summers, the director of the White House National Economic Council. Tapper, who was hosting that week, said: "Senator Kaufman is saying there isn't enough being done about too-big-to-fail. In 2000, you said: 'It is certain that a healthy financial system cannot be built on the expectations of bailouts.' Can you honestly say the Dodd bill changes that?" Summers replied, "Yes I can," and went on to enumerate three things that the bill would allegedly do, concluding, "Senator Kaufman is exactly right."

Two days later, we got a call from the White House that Summers (formerly Clinton's Treasury Secretary, president of Harvard University, and a hedge fund advisor) wanted to meet with Ted. Within the week, Summers came in and quickly settled into one of the chairs we'd drawn around the senator's coffee table. He was pleasant but wanted to dominate the discussion.

Ted would have none of that, and kept interrupting Summers with his own points, though doing so with a smile and a laugh. Ted was smart: although he wasn't going to let Summers lecture him, he sought to keep the meeting warm and friendly.

Summers made the same arguments to Ted that he'd been making in public. "Most observers who study this believe that to try to break banks up into a lot of little pieces would hurt our ability to serve large companies and hurt the competitiveness of the United States." Ted was prepared for that; he quickly cited Mervyn King, governor of the Bank of England, and Alan Greenspan himself. King had said: "Banks who think they can do everything for everyone all over the world are a recipe for concentrating risk." And Greenspan had admitted that Fed research "had been unable to find economies of scale in banking beyond a modest-sized institution." A decade ago, Greenspan had continued, "I noted that 'megabanks being formed by growth and consolidation are increasingly complex entities that create the potential for unusually large systemic risks in the national and international economy should they fail.' Regrettably, we did little to address the problem."

Summers's second argument was that, if we broke up the megabanks into smaller banks, "it would actually make us less stable. Because the individual banks would be less diversified, they would be at greater risk of failing because they wouldn't have profits in one area to turn to when a different area got in trouble."

He was essentially saying that, if banks are too big

to fail and we make them smaller, they'd be even more likely to fail (if they'd taken outsized risks). Maybe I missed it, but I've never heard or read anyone other than Larry Summers during Senate debate of the Dodd bill make this argument. Simon Johnson wrote of Summers's reasoning:

> I would not have a problem with the administration's top officials saying, 'we can't take on the biggest banks because (a) they are too powerful in general, and (b) they would cut us off from the campaign contributions that we need for November.' This would at least be honest. . . . But for the White House to make inaccurate claims regarding the views of 'most observers' is the most obvious and cheapest sham.

Ted remained more diplomatic than Simon, and the Summers meeting ended as a standoff: The administration was opposed to the Brown-Kaufman amendment, and Ted wasn't going to stop being a forceful advocate for it.

Secretary Geithner was next to ask for a meeting with Ted, though one would think that after Summers's experience, Geithner would've realized it was a waste of time. As we waited for Ted's previous meeting to break, I spoke to the secretary for a couple of minutes in the anteroom. He was far funnier and more relaxed than I would've predicted. Our banter had been so amiable that as I led him into Ted's office I jokingly assured Ted, "I've patted him down. He's clean."

Geithner said almost the same thing we'd heard earlier that year from Bill Dudley, the president of the New York Fed: We'll deal with too-big-to-fail banks at Basel and through capital requirements negotiated and synchronized with our regulatory counterparts at the international level. As Geithner had testified previously: "It is very important that these institutions . . . are subject to higher constraints on leverage in the future, more conservative cushions of capital and liquidity, so that they can absorb losses they face when they make big mistakes." Geithner wanted regulators free to set higher capital standards for the megabanks at the international level, so U.S. banks wouldn't be disadvantaged relative to foreign banks, and he strongly opposed the U.S. Congress taking a meat clever to them.

Ted had no confidence in the international capital standards process at Basel, and for good reason. In the past, it had failed; it had also been subject to national changes as the largest banks in each country asserted their political influence to negotiate lower capital requirements. As Ted said later on the Senate floor:

> I fear that, instead of putting in place strong structural reforms as a model for other nations, we are deferring too much to the discretion of regulators who have failed in the past and to international negotiations—currently under way in Basel, Switzerland—that have all too often

resulted in global standards that were the lowest common denominators.

Geithner, in a very polite way, complimented Ted's recent series of speeches but asked whether he could try to rebut them. He argued against specific size limits because risky but small institutions caused the crisis, noting that there was no correlation between size and risk in the crisis. He cited Lehman Brothers ($700 billion in assets), Bear Stearns ($400 billion in assets), Washington Mutual ($300 billion in assets), and Wachovia ($800 billion in assets). He added that Citigroup got in trouble largely due to "bad bets" on the mortgage market. He also used these points to try to demonstrate that Glass-Steagall had little to do with the crisis.

Ted said that the issue isn't only what happened in September 2008, but rather what will happen going forward. The Bank of England is very worried about incentives for excessive risk-taking in our largest banks. Why does Treasury think Mervyn King and Andrew Haldane of the Bank of England are wrong? Plus, one of our largest banks, Citigroup, failed, pure and simple. Bank of America made a huge miscalculation both in buying Countrywide and in acquiring Merrill Lynch (two very different kinds of transactions); and, like Citigroup, it would've failed without TARP and direct assistance from the Fed. Glass-Steagall is the inspiration for the Volcker Rule (on proprietary trading), Ted said, and President Obama and presumably the Treasury Department support the Volcker Rule. A cap on non-deposit liabilities, Ted argued, might be a simpler and better approach than the Volcker Rule, which could quickly get complicated.

After Geithner left, Ted and I chewed it over further. We believed that the financial crisis was such a disaster that we needed *ex ante* solutions, multiple failsafes to prevent it from ever happening again. Breaking up the largest megabanks, and thereby diminishing their political power and ability to capture future regulators, was the only certain way to prevent another crisis of similar—or perhaps greater—magnitude.

Finally, it was time for the full Senate to take up Dodd's bill. On April 27, Ted spoke to the caucus and said, "We should go right at the Republicans. As former senator Lawton Chiles used to say, 'It's a beautiful thing when conscience and convenience cross paths.' The public will be with us. No concessions." Senator Sheldon Whitehouse (D-RI) spoke next and urged the Democrats to "march around the bill seven times like Joshua at Jericho until the walls come tumbling down." Some Republican senators were bound to back down rather than risk looking like they were in Wall Street's pocket after the financial crisis.

In more than twenty years in Washington, I'd never followed a major bill through Congress as closely as I did the Dodd-Frank Act. In that time, I'd never fully grasped the almost absolute power to steer the bill wielded by committee chairs, especially when the leadership delegates all responsibility to them, as Harry Reid did to Chris Dodd. Almost nothing could happen on the Senate floor or get in the bill without Dodd's approval. That was particularly true in this case because Dodd and the Treasury Department wanted a squishy bill, and the Republicans were willing to work with Dodd to weaken it. (In the Senate, it takes unanimous consent for an amendment to come to the floor for a vote. So Dodd and Shelby had a vice grip on what amendments would be considered. They only accepted amendments they both liked.) On this bill, Shelby had never negotiated in good faith with Dodd. Indeed, Shelby had publicly and repeatedly said that he preferred no bill at all. Yet Shelby and the Republicans would cooperate by granting unanimous consent to Dodd's floor strategy, because they trusted that Dodd wanted to pass the weakest possible bill. And then the Republicans would still try to filibuster it.

Early in the Senate's consideration of the bill, I went to one of Harry Reid's staff, making the case that Brown-Kaufman deserved a debate and vote. He said, "Reid will only be for amendments that help Democrats up for reelection." And when other Democratic senators went to Reid about their amendments, Reid repeatedly said, "Work with Dodd." That's why the Senate first considered an amendment authored by Senator Barbara Boxer (D-CA); it consisted of precatory language stating that Congress would never again bail out failing banks (that is, until the next time Congress is forced to change its mind in a bail-out-or-go-into-a-Depression scenario). It was meaningless, but it helped Boxer in her Senate campaign for it to be a Boxer amendment.

Days dragged on with little Senate debate and few votes on amendments. Before long, almost two weeks had gone by. Dodd would dawdle and stall, blaming the Republicans for refusing to grant unanimous consent when Democrats wanted to offer amendments with teeth. I knew at some point Reid would come to the floor and say, "We've now been on this bill for three weeks, we need to file cloture and have a vote so we can move on to other pressing business." I began telling reporters the Senate was having a "fake" debate.

Ted was trying his best to convince Republican senators to break up the largest banks. He ran into Senator Tom Coburn (R-OK), who is very conservative. Coburn told Ted that he'd been reading about his speeches and would like to help. Later that day on MSNBC, Coburn said he was working with Senator Kaufman on an amendment. On May 1, at a dinner in Wilmington, the Republican Party state chairman came up to Ted and said he supported everything Ted was doing on financial reform. Ted talked to Republican Senators Isakson (R-GA), Barrasso (R-WY), and Johanns (R-NE), reminding them that they represent southern or western states, which from our country's founding have been opposed to the power of big banks. "It would be good for you politically if the front page of your hometown newspaper said 'Senator Votes to Break Up Big Wall Street Banks.'" They agreed with Ted on the politics, but said no. Senators McConnell and Shelby were working the Republican caucus very hard, demanding unity.

We pushed hard to get a vote on Brown-Kaufman. Then, suddenly, when it was clear to Dodd's vote counters that our amendment would fail (and before a weekend when the Greek debt crisis threatened to get worse, raising the specter of bank bailouts in Europe), Reid and Dodd scheduled a vote for that very night. Some have called it a "flash vote" because it was scheduled preemptively before we could gain any further momentum. Earlier that day, the flash crash had hit the stock market, vindicating Ted's months-long HFT campaign and enhancing his credibility with many of his Senate colleagues.

Reid said, "We all know the issues." We couldn't argue that Brown-Kaufman deserved a longer hearing. Since February 2010, Ted had orated tomes. Twice, Senators Brown and Kaufman had come to the floor and engaged in a dramatic colloquy, each playing off the other in their earnest desire to see the country protected from another financial crisis. On May 5, Senator Durbin stopped Ted on the Senate floor and said, "Jamie Dimon [the CEO of J. P. Morgan] asked me to tell you 'It was the small banks that failed.'" Ted went right back to the microphone and, without naming Dimon, said the Royal Bank of Scotland, which was bigger than any U.S. bank, had failed. The only reason our biggest banks like Citigroup didn't fail was because of TARP and support from the Fed. After Brown and Kaufman finished, they walked over to

Senator Dodd in the well of the Senate and jokingly asked him to accept their amendment. Dodd laughed and said no.

It was time to vote. Senators had to stand on one side or the other: Did you believe, as even Alan Greenspan belatedly had mused, "if they're too big to fail, they're too big"? Or did you believe, in effect, size doesn't matter? Ted gave a brief summation. Our argument was based in prudence. Whatever you thought had caused the financial crisis, it's clear that six megabanks have become so gigantic—and even more so after the consolidation that took place during the crisis—that they're too big to fail. If there's ever another crisis, these megabanks will be the recipients of a massive taxpayer bailout. The Fed has admitted that no economies of scale enable megabanks to help America better compete in a global economy—that's a false argument that banks make to preserve their ability to borrow at lower rates (because the markets perceive them to be government-backed). Why not place a statutory limit on their size and the amount of relative borrowing they can use?

No one could confuse the issue, at least I thought. But, just before voting, Senator Dianne Feinstein (D-CA)—one of the most liberal members of the Senate—asked Durbin, the majority whip, "What's this amendment?" According to Durbin, who later told Ted, he replied: "To break up the banks." Giving the thumbs-down sign, Feinstein said bemusedly: "This is still America, isn't it?"

Fifteen minutes later, the Brown-Kaufman amendment to break up the megabanks lay dead on the Senate floor, shot through by sixty-one no votes. Three Republicans—Richard Shelby (R-AL), Tom Coburn (R-OK) and John Ensign (R-NV)—joined 30 Democrats who voted for it. Most of the same senators who'd swallowed the novel idea of a $700 billion taxpayer-funded bank bailout just couldn't comprehend the idea of the government putting a size cap on any business. As Senator Judd Gregg (R-NH) had asked on the Senate floor: "What are we going to do next? Limit the size of McDonald's?" Last I checked, Big Macs hadn't collapsed, destroyed $20 trillion in housing and financial wealth, and thrown eight million Americans out of work. Under antitrust law, we stop businesses from combining if it leads to market power and consumer harm. Why can't Congress limit bank size to prevent financial instability and massive economic harm?

All along it had felt like "The Charge of the Light Brigade." For months Ted—cannon to the left of him, cannon to the right of him—had gone to the Senate floor to speak truth to power. *Time* called him "The Replacement Senator Giving Democrats Fits." Where was the rest of the cavalry? You'd think that senators would at least come to the floor and debate what role Wall Street had played in the disaster and what needed to be done about it. For a long time, Ted was the only one. It had been exhilarating as Ted galloped down the gauntlet, opposing the president, Larry Summers and Tim Geithner, Wall Street, the Delaware banks, and, most especially, the no-plan Republicans. He threw caution to the wind, cheered on by the media, his hometown *Wilmington News,* and many Americans (and, best of all, Delawareans). Then we reached the cannon line, vaulted it, were dismounted on landing, and lay in stunned disarray, knowing that for us and for now, the battle was over.

If it felt that way to me, imagine how it felt to Ted. He'd put his heart and soul into it, reaching deep inside for wisdom and eloquence ("stemwinders," one reporter called his speeches; even the *Guardian* called them "remarkable"). Senator Bob Corker (R-TN) said on the Senate floor, "I admire the senator for his passion." Another senator came up to him and said, "You're a regular Demosthenes." Ted could get quite angry, and yell, red-faced, "In the 1930s, our forebears in the Senate passed legislation that worked for three generations! We can't just pass it back to the regulators. . . . The buck stops here. In the Senate." I had watched at my desk on C-SPAN more than once and said, "He's like Biden." It was his finest hour.

Yet it was all over for the Brown-Kaufman amendment. After several drafts of a press release, I asked Ted, just returned from the stinging Senate floor defeat: "How do we start it?" He slumped into his chair and dictated: "I am disappointed." Not long afterwards, a senior Treasury official was quoted about the Brown-Kaufman amendment: "If we'd been for it, it probably would have happened. But we weren't, so it didn't."

Bill debate continued. Dodd started to tell Republicans like Scott Brown that he would "reasonably accommodate" Brown's concerns with the bill if Brown would vote for cloture (and gain the 60 votes needed to break the Republican filibuster). That gave Dodd license to further water down the bill behind closed doors and claim that it was necessary to gain Brown's vote. All of Wall Street lined up behind the Massachusetts banks to coach Brown on what changes to seek. Meanwhile, on the Senate floor, the amendments being considered were peripheral to the main issues.

Dodd was only wrong twice about an amendment's chance of passage. Dick Durbin had an amendment that would instruct the Federal Reserve to come up with a rule limiting interchange or "swipe fees" paid by merchants to Visa, MasterCard, and the credit card banks. No one thought it would get sixty votes. It hadn't been considered in a Senate hearing or in committee, but Durbin was part of the Democratic leadership, and there was a strong coalition of big merchants—WalMart and Home Depot among them—pushing for a vote and a win. Shockingly, Durbin got sixty-three votes and his amendment passed. That amendment proved that, when big business stands up for itself, Wall Street loses.

Similarly, Al Franken had developed an amendment that would establish a new federal commission to assign credit rating agencies to do the initial rating for a new financial product, so that Wall Street firms can't hire the firms that rate their products (and, potentially, shop for the firm that will give the best rating). It was such a common-sense idea that Franken's description of the amendment on the Senate floor persuaded ten Republicans to support it. It passed with sixty-four votes over Dodd's opposition (Dodd later drowned it in conference).

The Merkley-Levin amendment (the Volcker Rule) never even received a vote. The Republicans objected to unanimous consent. Determined to have their hour on the Senate floor, Senators Merkley and Levin offered their amendment as a second-degree amendment to a pending Republican senator's amendment. With this maneuver, the two amendments were linked together. The following day, cloture was invoked on the bill, making the Merkley-Levin amendment the next scheduled vote. Then, the Republican caucus convinced the Republican senator to pull down his amendment, bringing down the second-degree amendment with it—all to stop Merkley-Levin from getting a vote and passing. Dodd trotted out the same excuse he always used: "We can deal with it in conference."

When negotiations continued on the Merkley-Levin provision, Senator Merkley told Ted that he had negotiated with Scott Brown a "de minimis" exemption for fund investment that would allow banks to invest up to a 2 percent cap (reportedly a carve-out for State Street); yet Secretary Geithner and the Treasury Department were still pushing for an even weaker 3 percent cap. Dodd, of course, sided with Treasury over the weaker demand of Senator Brown, whose vote he needed—and so 3 percent went in the bill. I heard from other sources that the Treasury Department was taking a tougher line in negotiations than the Republican senators whose votes were in play.

Now Ted had to decide whether to vote for or against the final bill. Most of the reformer Democratic senators were unwilling to vote against cloture on the bill, which meant they had no leverage. Only Senators Cantwell and Russ Feingold (D-WI) voted no. Press reports portrayed Cantwell sitting with her arms crossed, a scowl on her face, as Dodd and Reid surrounded her on the Senate floor and tried to coax a yes vote from her. She was adamant. Feingold hadn't said much of anything until he suddenly walked forward and refused to vote for cloture. He was using his vote leverage too late. Even the Wisconsin press was on to him, and it ultimately hurt his reelection campaign, which he lost.

Neither Feingold nor Cantwell had ever appeared at the rump meetings called by Senators Dorgan, Levin, and Merkley to coordinate a push for stronger reform. At the final such meeting, the eight senators who did attend decided against opposing cloture or going public with a list of demands. Instead, they would talk privately to Dodd about two or three priorities they were determined to see added or preserved in conference. That proved to be a virtual capitulation in the name of Democratic Party unity.

Ted struggled with his decision on how to vote on the bill. At first he'd decided to make a symbolic no vote, since the bill would pass with at least 59 votes anyway. Then the idea of lining up with all the Republicans made him blanch. After talking to his wife, he voted aye.

The Senate-House conference was televised, but the final tough decisions on the Volcker Rule especially were a late night mugging perpetrated by the Treasury Department, Dodd, Barney Frank (D-MA), and Chuck Schumer. The rule was riddled with exceptions, and when Levin and Merkley, with some help from Senator Jack Reed (D-RI), tried their best to hold the line on the size of those exceptions, on the final night the leadership simply came in and said "this is what it's going to be" and gaveled the conference to a close.

Ted voted aye on the conference report, too, but not until he'd gone to the floor and flayed it. First, the bill punts too many decisions to regulators, Ted said. In the coming year, the bill mandates the regulators to undertake over two hundred studies and rulemakings, which threatens to overwhelm the ability of the SEC and CFTC to perform their essential oversight functions. Second, he said, the bill doesn't end too-big-to-fail. His concluding paragraphs were prophetic, and explained why a movement of citizen and businesses should insist on meaningful restraints on Wall Street:

> Many of the opponents of Wall Street reform make the dubious claim that the recovery is being held back by uncertainty about future regulations and taxes. In reality, it is being held back by the

financial shock and the fact that we are still in a period of financial instability and undergoing an excruciating process of deleveraging. Even now it is unclear whether a European banking crisis based on their holdings of sovereign debt will continue to impede that recovery. [We must] build a financial system on a firmer foundation. The American economy cannot succeed unless we restore and maintain financial stability.

Two years later, the largest European banks—the standard for why the United States needs its own mega-banks to compete globally, senators opposed to Brown-Kaufman had said—are still in crisis, causing continued financial instability. And the London Inter-bank Offering Rate (LIBOR)–fixing scandal has shown how rotten big-bank culture had become.

In time, Ted's words have gained even more force. That summer of 2010, though, public outrage was focused more on Washington than Wall Street. In October 1994, while I served in the Clinton White House, I don't remember anyone predicting a Republican blowout. This time, the only question was whether the hurricane blowing Democrats out of office would be a category four or five. As the Tea Party movement drove outraged voters to the polls by the millions, Democrats were swept out of office in historic numbers. And according to the Center for Responsive Politics, of the members who either retired or were defeated in 2010, of the seventy-nine who have found new employment, more than half now work in lobbying, for either a lobbying firm or a lobbying client. Since 2009, a Sunlight Foundation study shows that nearly four hundred staffers have left the House of Representatives to become registered lobbyists.

CONCLUSION

WITH ONLY WEEKS LEFT in Ted's Senate term, I received an e-mail from the staff director of the Permanent Subcommittee on Investigations asking me to fill in for her on a panel entitled, "Financial Crisis and Financial Crimes," held at the New York Fed on Election Day, 2010. It was an all-day seminar cosponsored by the New York District Attorney's office, and the organizers expected three hundred Wall Street attendees. This would be walking into the lion's den to talk about fraud at the heart of the financial crisis and the failure of federal law enforcers to prosecute it effectively. I sucked in my breath and agreed to go.

I was to follow Neil Barofsky, the Special Inspector General for TARP, himself no shrinking violet at poking Secretary Geithner and the Treasury Department. So I was emboldened that Barofsky would set the tone, and I could put the hammer down as hard as I wanted. On the other hand, I didn't want the speech to be a polemic, subject to counter-attack. It had to be factual and reasoned and not go beyond what I could defend. I was looking forward to giving a speech myself. Ted had tried his best to stay the most humble of men, but two years as a senator (this time with me always staying behind) had taken him to a higher plane. Now it was my turn to speak truth to power.

I opened with a joke about how I'd received two invitations for that day: one to speak on Wall Street about financial crimes and the other to help get out the vote in a tight Senate race in West Virginia. I said I'd thought about it, and I'd much rather be talking to Wall Street about fraud than going door-to-door in West Virginia (I'm from Alabama, and we never miss an opportunity to make a joke at West Virginia's expense).

Then, I launched into four questions. First, was there fraud at the heart of the financial crisis? Second, has the law enforcement response *so far* achieved effective levels of deterrence against financial fraud? Third, are federal law enforcement agencies sufficiently capable of detecting fraud and manipulation, particularly in markets that are increasingly complex? And finally, should Wall Street itself care about all this? In short, I said, my answers would be yes, no, no, and yes.

I wasn't far into my fifteen-minute presentation when I noticed you could've heard a pin drop. The audience was listening to me, as my points came straight and fast about how no American should believe that Wall Street is effectively policed. That the Justice Department evidently was failing where the Permanent Subcommittee on Investigations and the Lehman Brothers bankruptcy examiner had succeeded in putting together convincing evidence of fraud. That the SEC was letting firms off with parking-ticket fines rather than holding individuals accountable. That the regulatory agencies had fallen so far behind in monitoring increasingly complex trading markets that we have no systems in place even to detect what might be rampant manipulation by high-speed traders. And that after a devastating financial crisis, the flash crash, and a woefully inadequate governmental response, investors justifiably had lost confidence in whether Wall Street operates lawfully and their investments are dealt with fairly.

Then I came to my close: "Senator Kaufman's term, and my time as a Senate staffer, ends in twelve days, but this is not a fight for one senator to wage. These are questions that go to the foundations of the rule of law and America's future economic success. For the common good, I hope you answer them well."

As I walked through the crowd afterward toward the exit, every regulator in the audience—from the FDIC, HUD, and the New York District Attorney's office—came up and congratulated me. Among the Wall Street crowd, I heard two comments as I made my way to the door: "We appreciate someone coming here and not wasting our time." And: "That took guts." Afterward, I stood at the corner of Wall Street and Nassau and felt exhilarated. I called Ted. We did it. We had tried our best for two years. And by my lights I'd just told the clearest truths in the most effective way I could to Wall Street itself, in the New York Fed, no less. It felt good.

Another moment passed and another thought came to me, as I looked around and noted again just where I was standing. I didn't remember that Nassau was a downtown street, so prominent where it intersects with Wall, and wondered if I should move to the Bahamas. In reality, Ted and I had achieved very little. And, I thought, "Wow, I just blew myself up on Wall Street." I don't think I'll ever again be part of the Permanent Class. What will I do next?

When I decided to leave QGA to join Ted at the beginning of his Senate term, I had felt a diabolical tug. I thought I might pull my punches, go through the motions with Ted, be a managerial chief of staff, not upset any apple carts, solidify my reputation in town as a Biden guy, and then go right back to making big bucks while Biden was still vice president. If Ted and I weren't genuinely outraged that our system had failed so egregiously, that's probably what I would've done.

I felt the tug again as Ted's term was ending. I knew I could go back into lobbying, certainly back to QGA. And more and more lobbyists were working below the radar as solo practitioners, picking up a few clients at lower fee levels than those charged by the larger firms. Or maybe I could be the head of a DC office for a major corporation, one whose brand I could feel positive about. Then I envisioned my tombstone: "Jeff Connaughton, Corporate Lobbyist." I didn't want that to be my epitaph. And I was tired of pretending to be close to Biden. That's one fraud I could police.

When I was inside the lobbying world, I liked my

colleagues and clients (at least most of them), and it was easy to rationalize that I was advocating for reasonable positions. After all, we live in a capitalist economy, and each corporation is trying to maximize its value to its shareholders. Moreover, as a lawyer, I'm trained to be a zealous advocate for my clients. But it's one thing to be a frog in a pot on a stove that doesn't notice the water is getting hotter; it's quite another to jump back in when the water is at full boil. It was only after going back to the Senate and seeing how corporate interests completely overwhelm the public interest—in numbers, access, information, analysis, hiring through the revolving door, and most especially, fundraising—that it started making my stomach ache. While I enjoyed working at QGA and value greatly the friendships I made in lobbying, far more so than with the politicians I'd met, the system itself now seems deplorable.

This time, as the revolving door swung round, I knew the country was still suffering, while Wall Street banks had rebounded with taxpayer help, become profitable and bonus-laden again, and were, in my view, staggering inexorably toward yet another financial crisis. If I rejoined that system, it would be a conscious decision to put self over country. If I went back, it would be an act of pure greed, just to gild my personal lily.

Ted had wanted to start a not-for-profit to continue his work on financial issues, with me as the executive director. "I'll fight Wall Street," I told Ted, "But I'm not going to fight the Obama-Biden administration *and* Wall Street." The American people elected Obama and

Biden, and Obama had picked his regulators. Writing comment letters to those regulators and op-eds, staffing Ted as he continued the fight, just seemed inadequate. It was more of the same, operating on a losing scale when I already believed the Obama administration was hopelessly compromised on these issues. Tepid as the Democrats had been, the Republicans wasted no time urging Obama's former Wall Street funders to switch sides. When it comes to Wall Street, America has no meaningful two-party system of governance.

After twenty-three years in Washington I started thinking about leaving. I wanted out of Ted's shadow and didn't really want to return to Jack's.

Ted was receiving accolade after accolade. *60 Minutes* featured him in a story on the rise of high-frequency trading. He appeared on *The Daily Show* with Jon Stewart. E. J. Dionne wrote a fawning column urging President Obama to keep Ted working somewhere in his administration. Biden introduced him in Delaware as the "best two-year senator in the history of the U.S. Senate." It was typical Biden hyperbole, but Ted deserved the praise.

That same weekend, I visited my parents' house in Alabama. In all thirty years, my parents had never met Biden. But they'd written $1,000 checks for his campaigns in 1987, 1990, 1996, 2002, and 2008 and for his PAC in 2006. After I told my parents that I was leaving Washington to live in Savannah, my eighty-seven-year-old father said to me, "Biden never offered you a job? I can't believe after all those years of blood

and sweat for Biden he never even gave you a crumb."
I didn't even know how to put any context around that
for him, it's just too complicated. I'd learned the hard
way: loyalty for loyalty's sake is a fraud. I was guilty.

After that, I saw Biden only one last time. It was at
the Kaufman Senate good-bye party. Ted had already
received so much praise that I told everyone I wanted
the party to be about the staff, not Ted. We'd all worked
very hard, and we deserved a chance to pat each other
on the back. Someone must have leaked word to
Biden, because in the middle of my emotional farewell
toast to the staff, in walked the Vice President of the
United States. I kept speaking as though he weren't
there, while he and his entourage slipped quietly into
the back of the room. Then I introduced Ted for his
speech. Predictably, Ted handed things over to Biden.
And equally predictably, Biden went on and on about
how great Ted was and what a great senator he'd been.
And then Biden was gone. Off somewhere being vice
president, the second most powerful man in Washington. He didn't once mention my name and left without
shaking my hand.

In Washington, as a Professional Democrat, I could
count on the corporate marketplace to pay me for the
value I provided in access, insights, strategy, influence,
hard work and—most especially—results. In politics,
the box comes with no guarantee. When I finally
opened mine, it was empty.

EPILOGUE

FINALLY, WASHINGTON was in my rear-view mirror. I knew I needed a long break. I was tightly coiled with frustration, anger at the system, personal disappointment, and even cynicism about America's future. I had to unwind.

I spent a week in Costa Rica. In Mal Pais, I took a long, slow jog along the beaches and dusty roads that led to a two-acre hilltop overlooking the Pacific Ocean, the lot I'd bought in 2007 amid a speculative frenzy. But the global economic crisis had intervened, and I, like the buyers of the neighboring lots, had never broken ground. On the hilltop, I looked out at the ocean from my empty lot, my earthen savings certificate, now worth half what I'd paid for it. When I finally got back to my hotel room, I was so drenched with sweat and dirt that I stepped into the shower fully clothed and stood for a long time to soak myself with cool water.

Savannah, once I arrived, didn't seem much different. Yes, it teems with tourists—65,000 of them a day. But it also teemed with for-sale signs, sometimes three or four on a single block. I rented a carriage house attached to a mansion facing Forsyth Park, which is lined with beautiful live oaks draped with Spanish moss. My landlady and her husband had bought three houses before the crisis, back when real estate prices moved in one direction: up. Now two of the three were for sale, including the one with my rental unit. Others in the neighborhood faced similar fiascos.

During my first month in Savannah I felt like I was living in exile. I decided I needed to commit. So I dove in. I arranged to have my boat sent down from Maryland and soon made an offer for a big Victorian: two turrets, three stories, four baths, and nine rooms. It was twice the size of the house I'd just sold in Georgetown, and about half the price. I was benefitting from Savannah's burst real-estate bubble; I told my new neighbors I'd cashed in my Yankee housing dividend. The previous owners had at one time owned as many as four houses, I heard, but had gone bust and moved to Florida, where state bankruptcy laws enabled them to keep one homestead. The house in Savannah had been repossessed, and the bank wanted it off its books as quickly as possible.

My neighbors invited me to a circulating monthly potluck get-together. Each month, a different host supplied the drinks and refreshments, while the invitees brought a dish. I walked with my next-door-neighbors to the house of that month's hosts. They had a beautiful home. In Savannah, taste is refined, and I still haven't seen a house that doesn't look stylishly furnished and

comfortably decorated in soothing colors. The crowd
was mainly older people, in their sixties and seventies,
but with a tiny smattering of younger people. Everyone
was very nice, yet I felt like I'd parachuted into Savannah at an awkward in-between age. I missed the bright
young Kaufman staff and DC's young professional
scene.

I spoke to the host briefly, a man in his sixties, and
his wife, who was an interior designer. We made an appointment for the following week to talk about deco-
rating my house. A week later, I had to postpone our
appointment. Before I could reschedule, I ran into one
of my neighbors. He told me there was sad news about
the party host. I hadn't heard. The wife, he said, came
home and found him. He'd committed suicide. My
neighbor heard that he was overextended in real estate.
Savannah is a town near a beach that likes to throw
parties, but the undertow is strong.

Readjusting to normal life in Savannah was disori-
enting. In Washington, my Sunday ritual had been to
retrieve the *New York Times* and *Washington Post* from
my front stoop and sit down to watch *Fox News Sunday, Meet the Press, This Week,* and *Face the Nation.*
When the shows overlapped, I'd flip back and forth de-
pending on the guests. I'd read the papers during the
commercials and, after the shows were over, continue
reading into the early afternoon. This was the Sunday
ritual of virtually everyone I knew in Washington
(church-goers and parents of small children might tape
or TiVo the shows and watch them later, but that was

about the only variation). All this Sunday reading and viewing was essentially mandatory as a shared reference point for conversations with friends and colleagues for the rest of the week.

In Savannah, these same shows seem wildly irrelevant. Down here, people don't talk about national politics, except to say that Washington is clueless (the fact that I left is proof enough; no one ever asks me for details about DC). More importantly, seen from six hundred miles away, the shows seem like empty rituals. Rarely, if ever, does anything truly newsworthy transpire. Government officials use the shows as a platform to recite their talking points; the journalists and commentators, as a platform to ask supposedly tough questions. As I write this, the discussion is about potential Republican presidential candidates—nine months before the Iowa caucuses. In Washington, the topic must appear timely; in Savannah, it appears ludicrously premature.

After a few months in Savannah, I visited Washington for a long weekend. I socialized with more people in those four days than I had in the past four months. At one restaurant near Capitol Hill, I had drinks with friends and saw a parade of people like Tom Daschle, Harry Reid, and big-time lobbyists I knew. I even had coffee with a couple of reporters who are writing books about DC and who wanted to pick my brain. I now know why people like the easy drug of a fast-paced life and a feeling of being in the know, of belonging. If you reject your long-time professional culture, a giant hole appears. Now you need a new set of people, under-standings and things to do. Fortunately, Savannah is filled with the arts, music, film, theater, and opportu-nities for volunteer and charitable activities.

In Washington, I'd never had a dog. In Savannah, I'd be working at home, and my new house had a big courtyard. I went to the website of the Savannah Hu-mane Society and saw a three-year-old, medium-sized chow mix that looked nice but distressed. I decided to go meet her. They brought her out on a leash. She'd had a tough life, I learned. She'd been found in a back-yard with seventeen other dogs; the other sixteen were too feral and had to be put down. She'd seen the ugly side of life and hadn't forgotten it, plus she had heart-worm. But the staff assured me she was a sweetheart (she was the favorite of several of them), and something about her intrigued me. When I took her outside the shelter, she explored the area with her snout to the ground, a bit like she was trying to track down her lost mind. I sat cross-legged in the yard, and eventually she put her paws in my lap and rested her head against my chest. A wounded soul was reaching out to me. I'd found a friend.

I named her Nellie, and a few days after we were home, I noticed she was breathing rapidly. I typed into Google "how fast should a dog breathe?" and the an-swer came back, "About 70–80 breaths per minute." Nellie was breathing at least three if not four times a second. The web site also said respiration issues in a dog may be a symptom of heart failure. I tried to pet and calm her down. But she kept up at least 180 breaths a minute. I slept by Nellie's crate that night.

In the morning, before the vet's office opened, I got a call from Ted, asking me what I was up to. "Listening all night to a dog breathe." Then we were off to the vet, where Nellie got another X-ray, and the vet suggested it might've been an adverse reaction to the antibiotics. I took her off the medicine and within a day her respiration slowed considerably.

Now, I wake at sunrise each day to the sight of Nellie wagging her tail furiously. "Wanna go for a walk?" The park is a dog paradise, and Nellie (completely recovered) struts her stuff as she looks for squirrels. Once she sees one, she turns into a lioness, stalking forward slowly. She keeps her head, back, and tail perfectly level as she lowers her profile and creeps forward one step at a time. Nellie, once heartworm-infested, now has quite a vertical leap. If I give her enough slack, she'll sprint to the tree and take a mighty pounce. Once, we ran into a nest of five squirrels. Watching Nellie dart one way then another was as close to a Zen-like moment as I've had in years.

How easy it is once you've made it to insulate yourself from America's problems, to give up on changing an almost immutable Washington system. To believe the best lack all conviction, and the worst are filled with passionate intensity. To enjoy life wherever one lives as best one can while America continues on a path of decline. To despair that Wall Street and our government's inability to learn the lessons of a devastating financial crisis may have caused America's best days to be behind her, rather than hope Americans can find the ability to organize themselves to win back their democracy so that government works again for the greater good.

In the fall of 2011, the topics of Ted's Wall Street speeches in 2009 and 2010 are leading the news: unresolved questions about mortgage fraud on a massive scale; high-frequency trading blamed for unprecedented market volatility; fears about short-selling of European bank stocks lead to temporary short-selling bans in Belgium, France, Italy and Spain; too-big-to-fail banks in Europe and the U.S. starting to wobble, undermining the stability of the world financial system. The only difference is I'm hearing about it in Savannah, sometimes sitting with my chair pulled within a foot of CNBC-TV as I watch the markets rocket down (and up) with breathtaking speed.

In one week in August 2011, the Dow Jones moved up or down by more than 400 points a day for four straight days, the first time in our market's history we have ever experienced such sustained volatility. During the last five months of 2011, the average difference between the Dow's intraday high and low was a stomach-churning 260 points. New research suggests that high-frequency trading exacerbates volatility. But whatever the causes of the Dow's daily rollercoaster ride, millions of Americans are getting off it. Ordinary investors withdrew more than $135 billion from domestic stock mutual funds in 2011.

Now, as I write in the spring of 2012, the azaleas

and banking scandals are in bloom, including J. P. Morgan for failing to supervise complex derivatives positions by the "London Whale," one of its traders, leading to billions of dollars in losses. And worse, Barclays and other banks have been exposed for manipulating LIBOR, which sets rates for trillions of dollars of financial instruments, leaving the credibility of the banking community in tatters. In the summer of 2012, the stock markets went haywire again when Knight Capital was battered by its own software glitch and in 45 minutes lost $440 million. Americans in overwhelming numbers are losing confidence in our political system, financial system and financial markets.

What can America do to reclaim its government from the ruling financial elite?

First, Wall Street-Washington reform must become a cause that is loyal to neither party and that brings about an awakening among independent and Republican voters especially. Wall Street blew up and set in motion a chain of events that hastened America's fiscal and economic decline. We need to fix Wall Street (and Washington) so that that won't happen again.

Republicans, Democrats, and independents alike should realize that the American economy can't succeed without long-term financial stability and credible capital markets. Moreover, America's relative economic decline will continue if our best and brightest keep heading to Wall Street to engineer golden crumbs rather than create and build new industries and better products.

We need citizen power to stand up to politicians of both parties who refuse to hold Wall Street to account and bring about meaningful reforms. If you believe, as I do, that Wall Street's capture of Washington is America's biggest problem, it's time to stop voting for the lesser of two evils and stand on principle. The Occupy Wall Street movement for a time had been a refreshing gust of renewed hope for change. When will the Tea Party and Occupy Wall Street realize that, when it comes to crony capitalism, they share common ground?

We still need structural reform of Wall Street, either by separating federally insured commercial banking from risky investment banking by reinstating Glass-Steagall, or by passing Brown-Kaufman to place a size-and-leverage limit on too-big-to-fail institutions. We still need a Justice Department and SEC willing to enforce the law against the most powerful by holding accountable those individuals who are responsible for fraud. And we still need advanced regulatory surveillance capabilities to monitor increasingly complex trading markets where high-frequency computer strategies now run amok. We'll have none of those things until we break Wall Street's hold on Washington.

Second, voters must force these issues into the 2012 presidential campaign and every congressional election, this year and in future years. Unless President Obama makes a dramatic course correction, even Democratic voters who believe in reform should continue to stand up to him. There's nothing worse than a false prophet. The financial crisis was so cataclysmic, so devastating to the lives of millions of Americans, it had the potential to bring fundamental change to Washington. Instead, the "change agent" America elected president was compromised from the very beginning. Before Obama ever put his hand on the Bible—before he even won the election—he began handing the keys of power to the very financial elite who had brought about the cataclysm in the first place. Governor Mitt Romney's campaign, meanwhile, is gorging itself on Wall Street contributions, while Romney himself calls for the repeal of Dodd-Frank and makes blissfully amnesiac statements like, "I want regulators to see businesses and enterprises of all kinds as their friends, and to encourage them and to move them along." If the Republicans had had their way, the financial crisis would've led to no reforms at all, leaving Americans helpless to Wall Street offenses in a legal and regulatory system that had become a complete sham.

Under Obama-Biden, the SEC has made a small comeback and has finally adopted certain rules that Ted had pushed but that only begin the first steps to understanding high-frequency trading. For the most part, the SEC has remained on autopilot, refusing to buck the Wall Street players who camp in its hallways. (A study by Duke Law Professor Kimberly Krawiec reviewed federal agency meetings with outside parties to discuss the Volcker Rule posted between July 21, 2010, the date of presidential signing, and October 11, 2011, the date of rule proposal. It shows that financial institutions, financial industry trade groups, and law firms representing such institutions collectively accounted for 93.2 percent of all federal agency Volcker rule meetings, whereas public interest, labor, research, and advocacy groups and other persons and organizations accounted for only 6.8 percent.)

What's worse, the Obama Justice Department simply did not make a well-organized, well-resourced, and determined effort to hold Wall Street crooks to account. Apparently Rahm Emanuel and Secretary Geithner didn't want criminal prosecutions to disrupt the banking sector. Eric Holder, despite his swearing-in-day pledge, didn't care enough about upholding the rule of law. And Lanny Breuer was left to act like Eliot Ness in Kaufman's Senate hearings when in reality the bootleggers were getting away scot-free.

For me, what is deplorable is not the department's failure to bring charges, but its failure to be adequately dedicated and organized either to make the cases or reach a fully informed judgment that no case could be made. Given the inadequate effort, as President Obama virtually admitted in his 2012 State of the Union address when he announced the formation of yet another task force (which remains an ill-staffed farce), we'll never know what an appropriate effort would have produced. And that has resulted in the appearance of a double standard. If the explanation for the inadequate effort is corruption (the administration could not afford to anger Wall Street contributors), the revolving door, or a belief that the health of the financial industry is more important than legal accountability, then we have an actual double standard. I don't know the explanation, but in terms of faith in our institutions, it may not matter whether the double standard is real or apparent. That double standard has torn the social and moral fabric of our country in a way I find to be unforgivable.

Third, we must do something about getting money out of politics. I support calls for public funding of campaigns, but I simply don't believe it will happen. And even if Congress did pass meaningful limits, the Supreme Court, after decades of campaign finance jurisprudence, would likely strike down such a law as an unconstitutional limit on speech. For those reasons, some reformers are calling for a constitutional convention, but that would be opening a Pandora's box: a chaotic process with ideas for amending the Constitution not limited to campaign finance.

Although less ambitious, a movement to stop Congress from taking contributions from lobbyists would have a huge affect on the system. We should also ban lobbyists from bundling contributions for incumbent campaigns. Every good lobbyist I know would welcome such a change.

Until American voters reclaim Washington, The Blob will keep oozing along, bigger now than ever during the regulatory implementation of Dodd-Frank, as Wall Street further floods the zone with unprecedented legions of lobbyists, fundraising events, lawyers, analysts, and public relations professionals.

Every voter who wants to break Wall Street's hold on Washington should put congressional and presidential candidates to the test with two questions (in addition to shunning lobbyist contributions and bundling):

1. Will you agree not to take campaign contributions from too-big-to-fail banks and nonbanks? Don't stand idly by while too-big-to-fail institutions that will need Congress and the American taxpayer to bail them out when they fail—or else send us into another Great Depression—buy political influence. Politicians should pledge No on too-big-to-fail contributions.

2. Will you support a tiny user fee on Wall Street trades to pay for adequate oversight and enforcement?

A per trade fee would be specifically earmarked to construct a consolidated audit trail to allow better monitoring of trades and also strengthen the regulatory and law enforcement systems we need to prevent manipulation and wrongdoing. This isn't a tax for the general treasury; it's a user fee dedicated to policing Wall Street. For long-term investors, the fee would amount to pennies. For high-frequency traders who turn millions of trades per minute, it would take a serious bite out of their business model. We need to slow down the technical arms race that is leading to faster and faster trades without any corresponding social utility. MIT needs to be sending its graduate engineers to innovate our economy, not to find new ways to skim Wall Street profits.

Fourth, with respect to the revolving door, I support a one-year cooling off period for senior federal agency employees. If a lawyer worked at the SEC, she can go to a private law firm but for one year she should be barred from advising clients on SEC matters she touched. The assistant attorney general for antitrust can't leave and immediately start an antitrust practice. This is more than a ban on contacting one's prior agency for a year; it's a cooling-off period during which the departing federal employee can't earn money in a way that's directly related to his or her former job. Relatedly, I would greatly increase pay for regulatory staff. We need a corps of well-trained and competent regulators, and unless we make it a priority to recruit and retain good people, we'll never slow the revolving door.

Finally, we'll have another financial crisis. That will be the moment for this reform movement to clean house. People like Arianna Huffington, Simon Johnson, and Ted—and nonprofits like Better Markets and Americans for Financial Reform—already are leading the effort. Others from across the political spectrum have heard the call and will join them. In late July 2012, Sandy Weill—the quintessential mega-banker and architect of multiple financial mergers that led to Citigroup—shocked Wall Street when he called for the reinstatement of Glass-Steagall. It takes time, but the right ideas are gathering force. Although it would be nice to think a spontaneous movement like Occupy Wall Street can change Washington before it's too late, that's not likely. Reform probably will come from the rubble of the next financial catastrophe. As the Dodd-Frank Act was signed into law, Chris Dodd, Barney Frank, and Secretary Geithner didn't even pretend that we won't have another financial crisis, because they know videotape lasts a long time. The market meltdown of August 2011 may be a sign of debacles to come.

A true reform movement to break the Wall Street-Washington axis of greed may take a decade or more to succeed, until the next Teddy Roosevelt or FDR comes along. Both political parties are raising money from Wall Street with open baskets. Both parties continue to permit regulatory capture. And so the 2008 calamity, which should've brought about fundamental change, will be the prelude to the next financial disaster, under any foreseeable election outcome in 2012.

That's why all concerned people should get involved now.

ACKNOWLEDGMENTS

LIKE MOST OF WHAT I'VE WRITTEN in my career, this book benefitted from insights and comments added by a number of readers of earlier drafts. Foremost among these readers was Sean Ward, who worked tirelessly with me to polish the manuscript. Thank you as well to George Hodgman for substantial editorial advice. I also want to express my gratitude to Tim Trent and Bob and Lauren Tomhave for their comments, as well as friends in Washington who were extremely supportive and gave helpful feedback. Josh Goldstein, as usual, made a significant contribution to the chapters concerning high-frequency trading. My co-agents, Kathy Anderson and Jason Allen Ashlock, were invaluable in the process. Thank you to David Wilk and Prospecta Press.

Finally, I want to thank the staff of Senator Ted Kaufman, an extraordinary group of people, for their exemplary public service, and the many people I met in Washington—Democrats and Republicans alike—who are dedicated to making government work better for every American. And to Ted himself, of course,

without whose tenacious commitment to financial reform this book wouldn't have been possible.

ABOUT THE AUTHOR

JEFF CONNAUGHTON holds an MBA with honors from the University of Chicago and a JD from Stanford Law School. He worked for four years as an investment banker, first at Smith Barney and then at E. F. Hutton. In 1987, he joined Joe Biden's presidential campaign as Deputy National Finance Director and thereafter became his Special Assistant when Biden chaired the Senate Judiciary Committee. After graduating from Stanford, Connaughton clerked for Chief Judge Abner Mikva of the United States Court of Appeals for the DC Circuit, then followed Mikva as his Special Assistant when Mikva was appointed Counsel to President Bill Clinton. In 2000, along with Jack Quinn and Ed Gillespie, Connaughton founded Quinn Gillespie & Associates, one of DC's premier lobbying firms. He lives in Savannah, Georgia.